THE
SPACE
ATLAS

HEATHER COUPER AND NIGEL HENBEST
Illustrated by Luciano Corbella

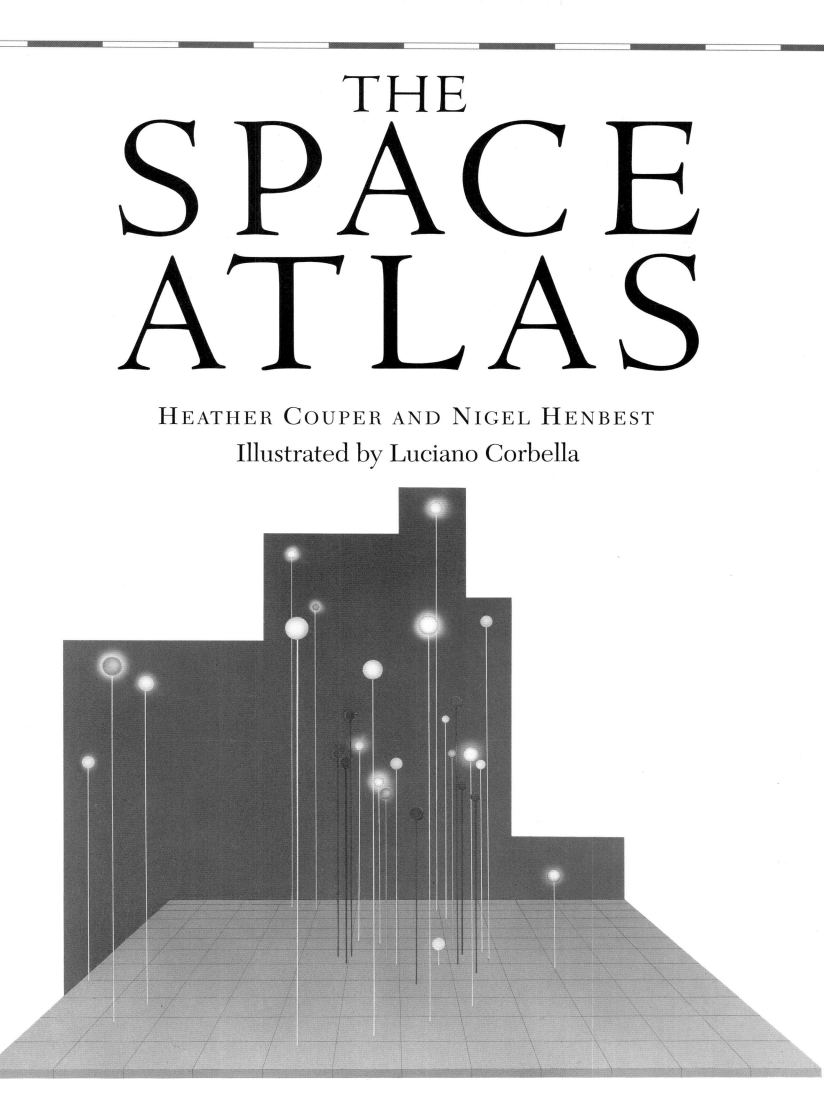

Gulliver Books
Harcourt Brace Jovanovich, Publishers
SAN DIEGO   NEW YORK   LONDON

HBJ

Art Editor Martyn Foote

Project Editor Jackie Wilson

Managing Editor Ann Kramer

Production Marguerite Fenn

Art Director Roger Priddy

Created by Dorling Kindersley Limited, London

Copyright © 1992 Dorling Kindersley Limited, London
Text copyright © 1992 Heather Couper and Nigel Henbest

First U.S. edition 1992

Library of Congress Cataloging-in-Publication Data
Couper, Heather.
The space atlas/by Heather Couper and Nigel Henbest.—1st U.S. ed.
p.   cm.
"Gulliver books."
Includes index.
Summary: An overview of the planets, moons, and other bodies
of the solar system, as well as distant stars, galaxies, and other
celestial phenomena.
ISBN 0-15-200598-6
1. Outer space—Exploration—Juvenile literature.
2. Solar system—Juvenile literature. 3. Astronomy—Juvenile literature.
[1. Outer space. 2. Solar system.
3. Astronomy.] I. Henbest, Nigel. II. Title.
QB500.22.C68   1992
520—dc20   91-24142

Reproduced in Italy by G. R. B. Verona
Printed and bound in Italy by New Interlitho, Milan

A B C D E

CONTENTS

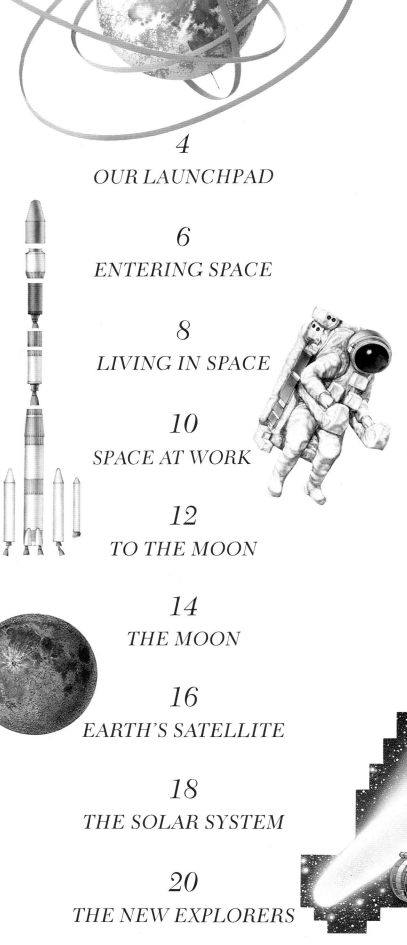

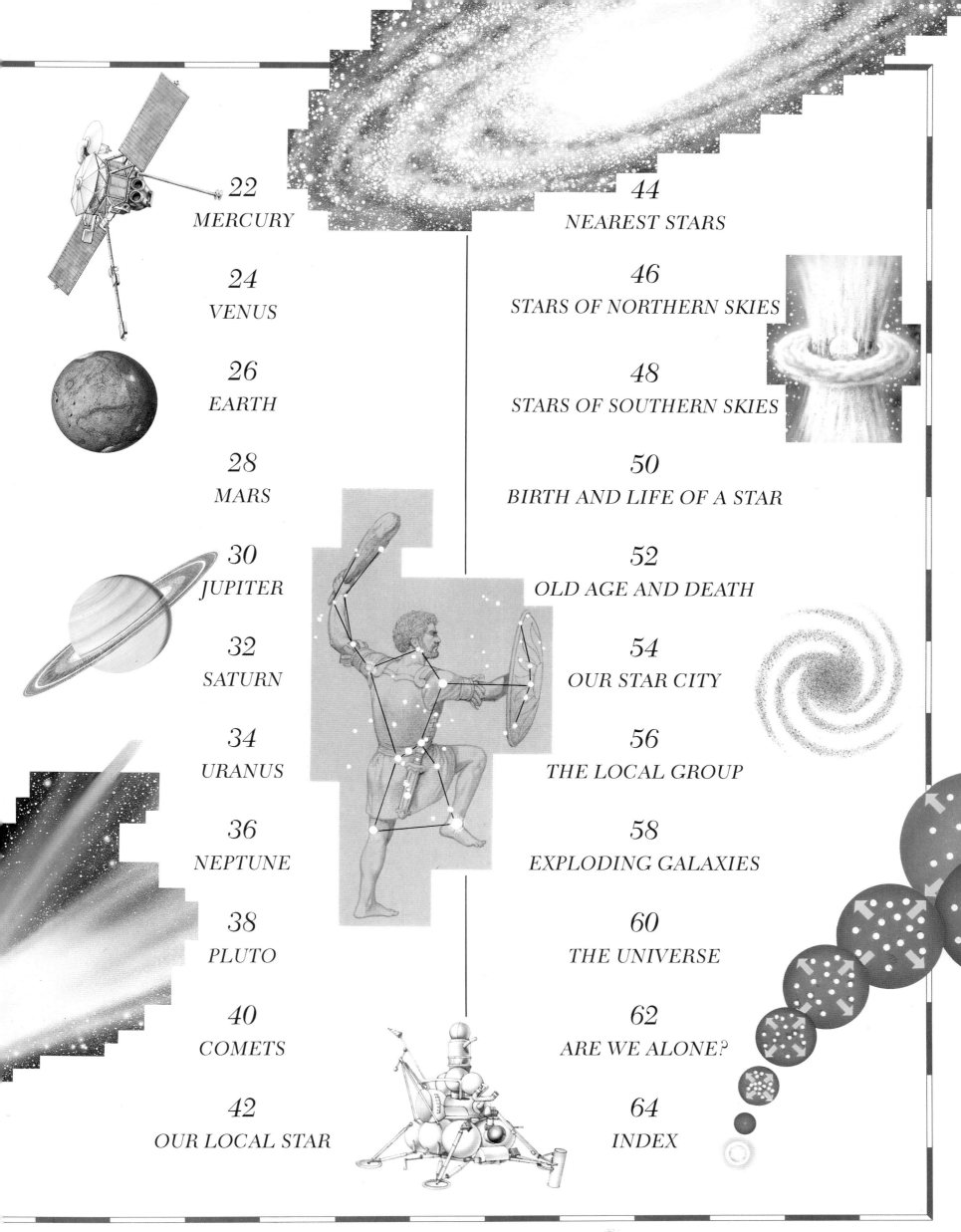

OUR LAUNCHPAD

MOST PEOPLE THINK OF AN ATLAS as a book containing maps of Earth. But Earth is just a small part of a much larger environment: the environment of space. Space may sound remote, but it is not far away. It begins about 150 kilometers up, where Earth's atmosphere thins out—the distance that some people travel every day. Things we take for granted—such as communications, weather forecasts, travel, and even what we read in the papers and see on television—would be very different if space were not part of our lives. And as time goes by, space is going to become even more important. This atlas looks at our environment on its largest scale, providing an overview of the Universe from the surface of Earth to the edge of space. Astronomers have been studying planets, stars, galaxies, and all the other celestial objects for centuries. But now they can investigate every aspect of the Universe using a wide range of sophisticated instruments—from giant radio dishes at sea level and powerful telescopes perched high on mountaintops to flying observatories and robot spacecraft that travel millions of kilometers to examine other worlds close up. All are precise and effective tools for unraveling the mysteries of the Cosmos. Planet Earth is where the journey to the edge of the Universe begins.

TUNING IN

One way of exploring the Universe from Earth's surface is by radio telescope. Many objects in space—particularly violent, distant ones such as exploding galaxies—give off energy in the form of radio waves that penetrate Earth's atmosphere and can be picked up by radio dishes. Radio waves are much longer in wavelength than light waves (hundreds rather than millionths of meters long), so radio telescopes must be much larger than optical telescopes to be able to "see" the same amount of detail. Australia's radio telescope at Parkes (*left*) is 64 meters across. Astronomers using radio telescopes have discovered many new kinds of objects in the Universe, including pulsars and quasars.

Springboard to the Universe

This map shows the world's most important observatories and launch sites, many of which are near the equator. Earth spins faster here and this gives a boost in velocity to spacecraft accelerating away from Earth's gravity. Optical observatories also gain from being near the equator: skies in these regions tend to be clearer and, during the course of the year, they are able to view the stars of both southern and northern hemispheres. Radio telescopes, however, can "see" through cloudy skies, and many are located farther north and south, in countries such as Germany and Australia.

 Launch centers

Optical observatories

Radio telescopes

AIRBORNE OBSERVATORY

The Kuiper Airborne Observatory (KAO) is a converted transport aircraft dedicated to observing the sky at infrared wavelengths. Many objects in space give off infrared radiation, which cannot pass through Earth's atmosphere. The KAO flies at 13,000 meters, above most of the air, where its 0.8 meter telescope can detect infrared radiation easily. In 1977, the KAO discovered the rings around the planet Uranus.

Lick
Owens Valley
Vandenberg
Mt. Hopkins
Palomar
Kitt Peak
Mauna Kea
Socorro
Yerkes
Greenbank
Cape Canaveral
Arecibo
Kourou
Las Campañas
La Silla
Cerro Tololo

The scale of space
The strip along the top of these pages shows the relative heights above sea level of some famous observatories. On later pages, the top strips—always to scale—take us from Earth to the most distant galaxies and quasars.

EYES ON THE SKY

The human eye was our first instrument for observing the Universe, and optical telescopes are just larger versions of the eye. But while the collecting area of the eye, the pupil, is at most 8 millimeters across, the collecting area of a telescope, the mirror, can be very big indeed. The telescope on the left of this picture, at Kitt Peak National Observatory in Arizona, has a mirror that is 2.2 meters across; the telescope on the right has a mirror 4 meters in diameter. Keck Telescope in Hawaii, the biggest telescope in the world, has a mirror 10 meters across. Big mirrors collect an enormous amount of light and can detect objects millions of times fainter than the eye. They can also "see" much finer details. Astronomers no longer look through their telescopes: electronic detectors, which are far more efficient, feed their data directly into computer memory for later analysis or for processing images.

GOING THERE

In the past 25 years, we have been able to explore the Universe up close. The *Titan* rocket (*above*) and other launch vehicles have sent dozens of spacecraft beyond Earth. Probes have studied all the planets except Pluto at close range. Spacecraft have landed on Mars and Venus, and astronauts have walked on the Moon. In the next century, more people will have the chance to explore the Solar System when colonists from Earth set up bases on the Moon and Mars. These bases will be springboards for future journeys to the stars.

Plesetsk

Jodrell Bank
Cambridge
Effelsberg
Nançay   Crimea
Calar Alto
La Palma

Kapustin Yar
Zelenchukskaya   Baikonur

Jiuquan

Kagoshima   Nobeyama
Tanegashima

Xi Chang

Sriharikota

San Marco

Sutherland   Hartebeesthoek

Siding Spring   Narrabri
Parkes

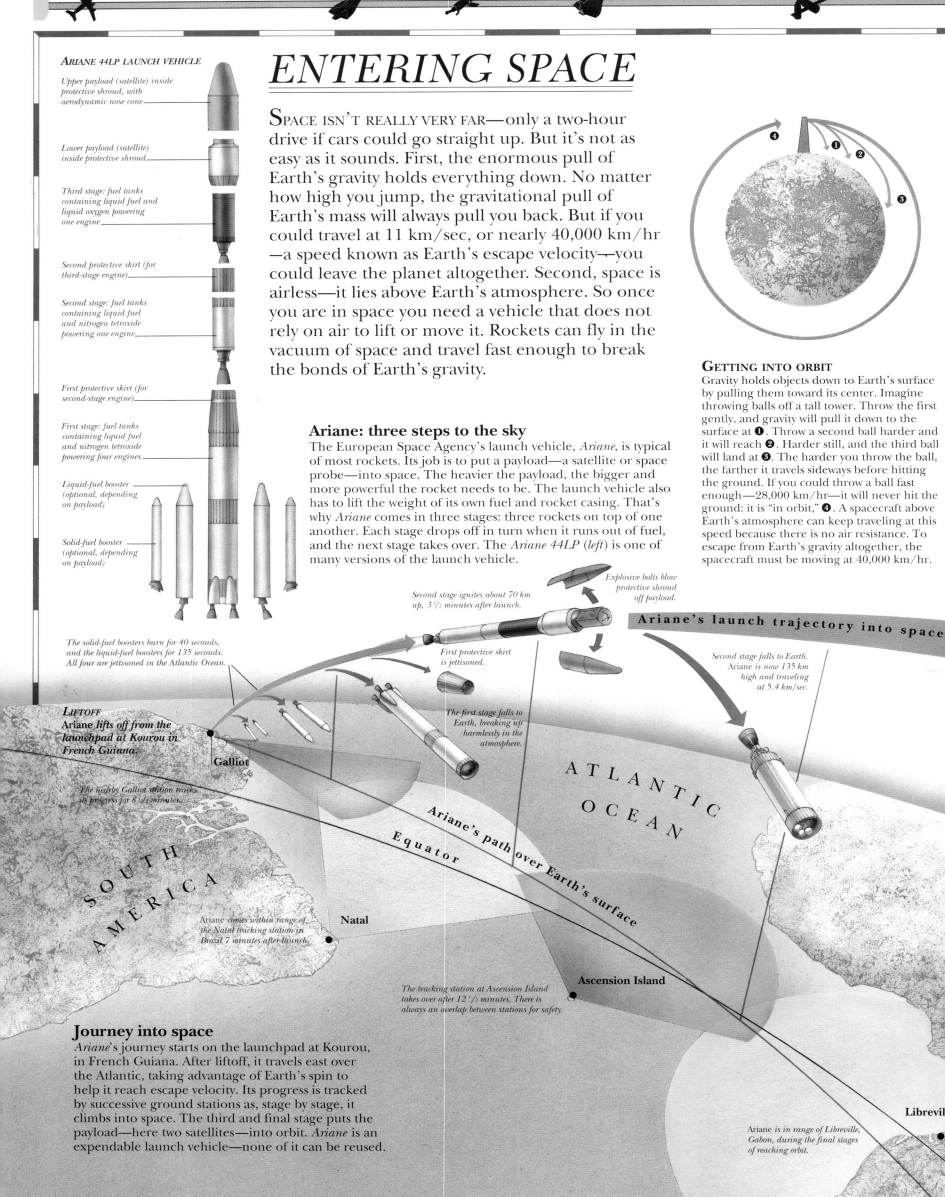

ENTERING SPACE

SPACE ISN'T REALLY VERY FAR—only a two-hour drive if cars could go straight up. But it's not as easy as it sounds. First, the enormous pull of Earth's gravity holds everything down. No matter how high you jump, the gravitational pull of Earth's mass will always pull you back. But if you could travel at 11 km/sec, or nearly 40,000 km/hr —a speed known as Earth's escape velocity—you could leave the planet altogether. Second, space is airless—it lies above Earth's atmosphere. So once you are in space you need a vehicle that does not rely on air to lift or move it. Rockets can fly in the vacuum of space and travel fast enough to break the bonds of Earth's gravity.

Ariane: three steps to the sky

The European Space Agency's launch vehicle, *Ariane*, is typical of most rockets. Its job is to put a payload—a satellite or space probe—into space. The heavier the payload, the bigger and more powerful the rocket needs to be. The launch vehicle also has to lift the weight of its own fuel and rocket casing. That's why *Ariane* comes in three stages: three rockets on top of one another. Each stage drops off in turn when it runs out of fuel, and the next stage takes over. The *Ariane 44LP* (*left*) is one of many versions of the launch vehicle.

GETTING INTO ORBIT

Gravity holds objects down to Earth's surface by pulling them toward its center. Imagine throwing balls off a tall tower. Throw the first gently, and gravity will pull it down to the surface at ❶. Throw a second ball harder and it will reach ❷. Harder still, and the third ball will land at ❸. The harder you throw the ball, the farther it travels sideways before hitting the ground. If you could throw a ball fast enough—28,000 km/hr—it will never hit the ground: it is "in orbit," ❹. A spacecraft above Earth's atmosphere can keep traveling at this speed because there is no air resistance. To escape from Earth's gravity altogether, the spacecraft must be moving at 40,000 km/hr.

ARIANE 44LP LAUNCH VEHICLE

Upper payload (satellite) inside protective shroud, with aerodynamic nose cone

Lower payload (satellite) inside protective shroud

Third stage: fuel tanks containing liquid fuel and liquid oxygen powering one engine

Second protective skirt (for third-stage engine)

Second stage: fuel tanks containing liquid fuel and nitrogen tetroxide powering one engine

First protective skirt (for second-stage engine)

First stage: fuel tanks containing liquid fuel and nitrogen tetroxide powering four engines

Liquid-fuel booster (optional, depending on payload)

Solid-fuel booster (optional, depending on payload)

Second stage ignites about 70 km up, 3½ minutes after launch.

Explosive bolts blow protective shroud off payload.

Ariane's launch trajectory into space

The solid-fuel boosters burn for 40 seconds, and the liquid-fuel boosters for 135 seconds. All four are jettisoned in the Atlantic Ocean.

First protective skirt is jettisoned.

Second stage falls to Earth. Ariane is now 135 km high and traveling at 5.4 km/sec.

LIFTOFF
Ariane lifts off from the launchpad at Kourou in French Guiana.

The first stage falls to Earth, breaking up harmlessly in the atmosphere.

Galliot

The nearby Galliot station tracks its progress for 8½ minutes.

ATLANTIC OCEAN

Ariane's path over Earth's surface

Equator

SOUTH AMERICA

Ariane comes within range of the Natal tracking station in Brazil 7 minutes after launch.

Natal

The tracking station at Ascension Island takes over after 12½ minutes. There is always an overlap between stations for safety.

Ascension Island

Journey into space

Ariane's journey starts on the launchpad at Kourou, in French Guiana. After liftoff, it travels east over the Atlantic, taking advantage of Earth's spin to help it reach escape velocity. Its progress is tracked by successive ground stations as, stage by stage, it climbs into space. The third and final stage puts the payload—here two satellites—into orbit. *Ariane* is an expendable launch vehicle—none of it can be reused.

Libreville

Ariane is in range of Libreville, Gabon, during the final stages of reaching orbit.

External fuel tank containing liquid hydrogen and liquid oxygen

Solid-fuel rocket booster

Space Shuttle orbiter

Space Shuttle: the reusable launch vehicle

Launching satellites by rocket is expensive because the rocket is effectively destroyed by the process. The U.S. Space Shuttle is an attempt to cut the cost of space travel by making most of the launch vehicle reusable. At liftoff, the Shuttle is pushed into space by two solid-fuel booster rockets that produce a brief but powerful thrust. The spent boosters then parachute into the ocean, where they are recovered and reused. The only part of the system that is destroyed is the large fuel tank, which feeds the Shuttle's own engines. The tank is jettisoned 8 minutes into the flight, by which time the Shuttle is in space. In the course of a mission, which usually lasts a week, the astronauts can launch several satellites, do experiments in space, and even repair damaged satellites in orbit. After the mission, the Shuttle, protected by hundreds of heat-resistant tiles, reenters the atmosphere and coasts back to Earth like a glider.

Touchdown! After a successful mission, Space Shuttle Atlantis *touches down on the dry bed of Rogers Lake in California. Even on landing, the Shuttle is traveling at a speed of about 350 km/hr.*

As large as an aircraft, the Space Shuttle lifts off with a power equivalent to 140 jumbo jets. NASA now has four vehicles in its shuttle fleet: Atlantis, Columbia, Discovery, and Endeavour (Challenger was destroyed in an accident in 1986). Each orbiter can carry a crew of eight and fit a payload of 29,500 kg in the 18.3-meter-long cargo bay.

SÄNGER
This proposed German spaceplane consists of two stages: a conventional "carrier" aircraft and a reusable space vehicle, Horus.

Spaceplane

Conventional aircraft cannot travel in the vacuum of space because their engines must take in air to work. Several nations are now engaged in developing spaceplanes. These would take off horizontally, like a normal plane, and use air while still within Earth's atmosphere. On reaching the threshold of space, their engines would then switch to rocket-mode so that they could operate in a vacuum while in orbit. The space-plane engines being developed are still highly secret, but such planes will probably be able to travel at up to 25 times the speed of sound (Mach 25) and be able to carry passengers from London to Sydney in just two hours.

Stage-three engines burn for about 12 minutes. When Ariane reaches its target orbit, the engines switch off.

A maritime communications satellite is about to be released. The second satellite, housed in the cylinder behind, will be launched later.

Second protective skirt falls to Earth as third stage ignites.

HOW A ROCKET WORKS

Rocket engines are an excellent demonstration of the principle that every action has an equal and opposite reaction. Liquid hydrogen and liquid oxygen mix in a chamber where they create a continuous explosion. This exerts tremendous pressure on the walls of the chamber, except at the rear where exhaust gases are allowed to escape through a nozzle. There is, however, a strong force on the front of the chamber. This force—the reaction to the pressure of the hot gas—pushes the rocket forward.

Exhaust gases escape through nozzle

Combustion chamber

Unbalanced force pushes rocket forward

Liquid hydrogen

Liquid oxygen

A rocket is propelled entirely by the thrust of its escape gases—like a balloon with its mouth open—and does not need air to push against. In fact, it works best in a vacuum.

FINE TUNING

A satellite will need to make minor changes in position—for instance, to "lock" on a star for navigation. It does this by firing small rocket thrusters, which make tiny shifts in its orientation.

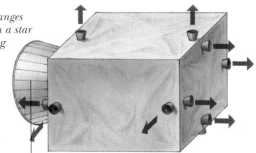

Main rocket engine for changing orbits

Small thrusters point different ways to give movement in any direction

A F R I C A

LIVING IN SPACE

THE FIRST TRIPS BY ASTRONAUTS INTO SPACE, in the 1960s, were brief hops lasting only a few hours. But when the U.S. challenged the Soviet Union to place a man on the Moon before the end of the 1960s, spacecraft became more sophisticated, and astronauts spent more time in them. After the Moon race (in which the U.S. emerged as victor), there was a change of heart. Both countries saw astronauts as an expensive (and dangerous) luxury in space. To justify their place on board, astronauts had to become cost effective. Space changed its image—from a stage for heroic deeds and "star wars" battles, to a platform for testing new techniques in manufacturing. The Soviets pioneered the way by developing *Salyut* and *Mir*, space stations where cosmonauts, as Soviet astronauts are called, could carry out experiments lasting weeks, months, or even years. The U.S. has done shorter experiments on the Space Shuttles, and is now building its own space station. But all this means living in space for long periods. How will people cope?

Doctor in space: U.S. astronaut Shannon Lucid checks the blood flow of her colleague Donald Williams, mission commander of the Space Shuttle Atlantis *during a flight in 1989. In the weightless conditions of space, blood and other body fluids do not know which way is "down" (see below).*

HATCHWAY
A cosmonaut checks the heavy door that seals the entrance of the airlock to the Soyuz docking port.

MAIN CONTROL DESK
Cosmonauts monitor and control Mir's systems from this desk. It is a tight fit because this is the narrowest part of Mir, but they spend only short periods of time here.

Kvant-2: *a service module that contains a large airlock and equipment to assist cosmonauts doing outside repairs.*

HANDRAILS
Cosmonauts working outside are tethered, or wear a "manned maneuvering unit," but a handrail helps them to stay in position and move around the station.

Solar panel: *this bulky item arrived at Mir folded, to be unfurled when in position. It helps keep the station supplied with energy.*

Soyuz: *a ferry craft that takes crews up to Mir. It can carry two or three people into space.*

Kvant: *an astronomical module, where instruments can carry out observations that are impossible from Earth's surface.*

WEIGHTLESSNESS
Cosmonauts float around as if there is no gravity, because both they and Mir are "falling" at the same rate as they orbit Earth: they are apparently weightless.

Kristall: *a module designed for experiments in processing materials. In space, you can make very pure and reliable semiconductors for use in electronic circuits.*

Main module: *the cosmonauts live and work in this 13-meter-long module, often for many months.*

Progress: *an unmanned cargo craft that ferries supplies to and from Mir.*

Docking module: *this module is designed for Buran, the Soviet "space shuttle," to dock with Mir.*

MIR
Building a space station on Earth and then putting it into orbit would be impossible: the structure would be too large and heavy. It's much easier to build one in space using modules that fit together—like the Soviet *Mir* space station. The basic *Mir* module, launched in 1986, has six docking ports so that a range of other modules can be connected as time and money allow.

Can we live in space?
Some cosmonauts have spent more than a year on *Mir*, but living in space is not all that easy. Nearly half of spacefarers suffer "space sickness"—a kind of dizziness and nausea—when they first experience weightless conditions. Most, though, soon adapt to the new environment. More serious is how the liver, heart, and other vital organs react to the change in circulation of blood and other body fluids. However, the flow of fluid to the face does make astronauts look, temporarily, younger. But muscles start to waste, and astronauts must exercise to combat this. Most dangerous is the loss of calcium, which can weaken bones. Perhaps just as serious is the psychological effect of very long space flights—this is still unknown, but could rule out long trips to the planets.

The astronaut needs a spacesuit that is highly protective when he or she works outside the Shuttle. This one is made of layers of three artificial fibers—nylon, Dacron, and Kevlar—and should last for 15 years.

As well as all its gas nozzles and controls, the MMU has three positioning lights, a gyroscope, and an automatic TV camera.

The MMU propels the astronaut through space by means of 24 small gas nozzles.

Manned Maneuvering Unit

The Manned Maneuvering Unit, or MMU, turns an astronaut into a self-contained spacecraft. The original MMU was designed for the U.S. Space Shuttle, but Soviet cosmonauts now use a similar unit. Shaped like an armchair, the unit is 125 cm high and weighs 100 kg. It attaches to the back of a spacesuit, and has two arms containing all the controls. Using these controls, the astronaut can move in any direction at speeds of up to 20 m/sec. The thrust comes from small nozzles which squirt nitrogen from two high-pressure tanks. There is enough nitrogen in the tanks for several circuits around the Shuttle, and the tanks can be refilled inside the Shuttle itself.

Which way is up?
Floors and ceilings are different colors to help the cosmonauts orient themselves.

Sleeping in space
Cabins have vertical sleeping bags—it doesn't matter which way you lie when there's no gravity pulling you down.

Communications
The smaller antenna (left) communicates with craft about to dock, while the larger one (right) relays messages to satellites when Mir is not directly above a receiving station on Earth.

Rocket motors
These are fitted to Mir to make small corrections to its position in orbit.

Docking port
Originally used for visiting Soyuz and Progress craft, this port is now occupied permanently by the Kvant astronomy module.

Working out
Weightlessness is bad for the bones and muscles, so spacefarers must strengthen them by exercising for long periods—on either a moving walkway or an exercise bicycle.

Space Station Freedom

A new space station, Freedom, will soon begin to take shape in orbit around Earth. Like Mir, it is put together from modules. The basic space station consists of four pressurized modules strung from a 145-meter boom that also carries the enormous solar panels. One of the modules will house the crew (of up to eight), while the others will be laboratories. Freedom is an international project. It is led by the U.S. in partnership with Canadian, Japanese, and European space organizations. Some will contribute laboratories to be attached to the space station. Research on Freedom will concentrate on biological experiments and processing materials because, in space, you can produce very pure drugs and electrical components. There will also be independent—or free-flying—modules in orbit alongside Freedom and platforms in polar orbit around Earth. These will provide further scientific facilities, and be serviced from the space station. One day, Freedom could be a launchpad for journeys to Mars.

Four pressurized modules, 13-m long by 4-m high, form the heart of Freedom. Each is large enough to accommodate the payload from a single Space Shuttle.

Europe's Columbus module (left) and the Japanese Experiment Module (right). Both are pressurized, so astronauts working inside the laboratories do not have to wear spacesuits.

Power from the Sun: the main lattice structure carries the modules and the huge solar panels. These are 27-m long by 10.5-m wide, and can generate 75 kilowatts of power.

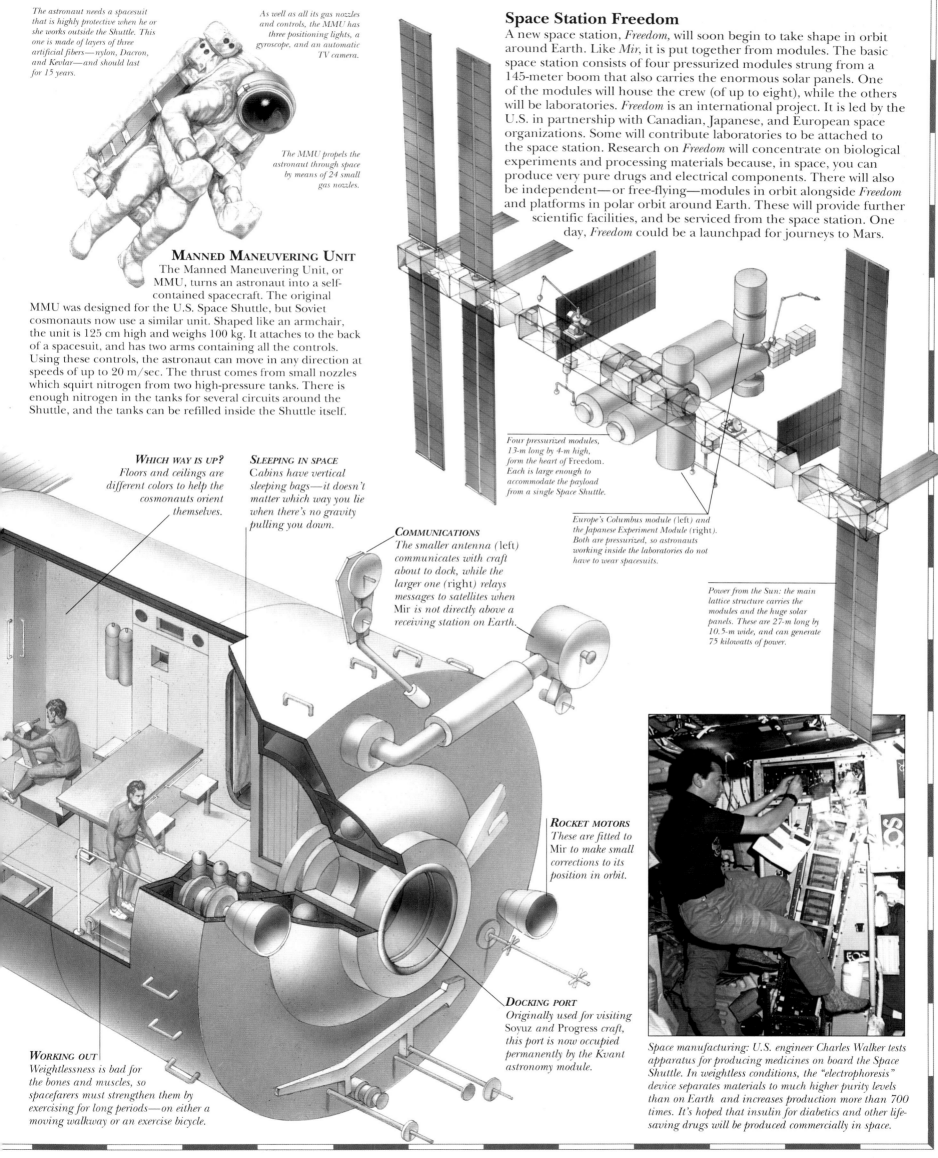

Space manufacturing: U.S. engineer Charles Walker tests apparatus for producing medicines on board the Space Shuttle. In weightless conditions, the "electrophoresis" device separates materials to much higher purity levels than on Earth and increases production more than 700 times. It's hoped that insulin for diabetics and other life-saving drugs will be produced commercially in space.

SPACE AT WORK

SATELLITES ARE LAUNCHED for a very practical reason: to benefit us. A few satellites carry out scientific research, but most contribute to the quality of our lives. For example, 30 years ago, international phone calls were virtually unheard of, and TV stations relied on aircraft to bring the latest news pictures from the other side of the world. Today, communications satellites can send thousands of phone calls and dozens of TV channels simultaneously. Other specialized satellites also make our lives easier— by forecasting the weather, assisting planes and ships with navigation, or locating deposits of oil and other valuable minerals. Launching satellites is expensive, but the "eyes in the sky" have proved their value.

San Francisco Bay from space: this Landsat *image shows several bridges, including the Golden Gate (top left). The colors in the water are caused by different types of algae.*

LANDSAT

The U.S. *Landsat* program has been running since 1972. The two most recent satellites, each the size of a family car, circle Earth in polar orbits, crossing over the entire planet as it rotates. *Landsat* images are used in making surveys of minerals, checking forest growth, investigating disaster areas, and for other purposes.

CHANGING ORBIT
A communications satellite moves to a higher orbit after launch from the Space Shuttle. The satellite has a rocket motor that gives it the boost it needs to reach its target orbit.

TELESCOPE IN SPACE
The first telescope in orbit, the Hubble Space Telescope, *unfortunately has a warped mirror. But computers can correct for many of the distortions. Above the blurring effect of Earth's atmosphere, the telescope has a clear view of the Universe.*

EARLY WARNING
A U.S. missile-warning satellite equipped with an infrared sensor, which can detect the hot exhaust from a nuclear missile. Other military satellites carry cameras so powerful that from orbit 150 km away, they can see a person on the ground.

OVER SOVIET SKIES
The Molniya, *a communications satellite, travels in an "eccentric orbit" that keeps it above the USSR for longer than other orbits.*

❷ NAVSTAR

❸ SHUTTLE

❶ IRAS

Molniya

KEEPING AN EYE ON THE PLANET'S WEATHER

Weather satellites are the most successful of the "eyes in the sky." From their vantage point in space, they can see weather patterns. A satellite in orbit can easily see how the clouds are moving, and weather forecasters use this information to predict the weather for days ahead. Such accurate forecasts are vital to farmers, particularly in regions of the world that have an unpredictable climate. It means farmers can allow their crops to ripen for as long as possible and harvest them just before rain or high winds move in. Weather satellites can also see hurricanes coming, giving authorities time to evacuate people and to take other safety measures. Forecasts for farmers and hurricane warnings have saved so much money that weather satellites have repaid their cost many times over.

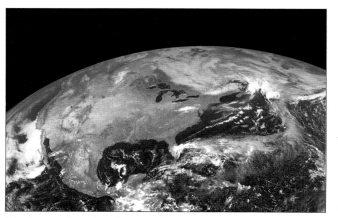

Weather watch: a clear day over North America, as recorded by one of the two GOES *craft (Geostationary Observational Environmental Satellite). Each craft hovers over a different point on Earth's surface.*

IUE
The International Ultraviolet Explorer *is an astronomical satellite studying ultraviolet radiation from space. Launched in 1978, and still working, the IUE has made hundreds of discoveries and even allowed astronomers to "weigh" a black hole.*

METEOSAT
One of the satellites in Europe's weather satellite system, this Meteosat craft hovers over the Atlantic Ocean. From there it can monitor weather systems approaching Europe from the west, as well as following conditions in the Mediterranean.

COMSTAR
One of a series of U.S. communications satellites in geostationary orbit. The most advanced Comstar can relay 18,000 phone calls over the whole of the U.S., including Alaska and Puerto Rico. The two "owl's eyes" on top of the 5-meter-high craft are antennas for receiving and transmitting signals.

❶ IRAS
A satellite designed to pick out sources of infrared (heat) radiation in space, IRAS discovered 250,000 new astronomical objects. These included stars being born, dusty comets, and violent galaxies.

❷ NAVSTAR
One of a network of U.S. satellites that have revolutionized navigation. Boats and planes can pick up the satellites' signals, which tell them their position to within 100 m or less, no matter where they are on Earth.

❸ SHUTTLING INTO SPACE
The U.S. Space Shuttle travels only in low Earth orbit—about 300 km up. At this altitude, however, it can service and repair many satellites. It can also launch satellites into different orbits.

Diagram not to scale

GEOSTATIONARY ORBIT
The time a satellite takes to circle Earth depends on the height of its orbit—the lower the orbit, the faster the satellite has to go to resist the pull of Earth's gravity. A satellite placed 35,880 km above the equator is described as being in geostationary orbit, because it orbits in exactly 24 hours—the same time that Earth takes to spin on its axis—and appears to hover over one point on Earth's surface. Three communications satellites, spaced evenly apart in geostationary orbit, can view the entire globe.

Geostationary orbit

Polar orbit

Eccentric orbit

WHICH ORBIT?
Satellites are placed in different orbits depending on the job they have to do. The easiest orbit to reach is a low orbit (about 300 km up), which is where the Space Shuttle and the Soviet space station *Mir* orbit. A polar orbit circles north-south over the two poles. This is the preferred orbit for survey and spy satellites, because they can cover the whole globe as Earth turns. The Soviets often favor eccentric orbits for their satellites, because a craft in this type of orbit will spend a lot of time above their country. Weather and communications satellites use geostationary orbits, so that they can hover over a large area.

Low Earth orbit

ACTIVITIES

● See if you can spot a satellite. Just after sunset, or before sunrise, they reflect the Sun's light. There are dozens of satellites in orbit bright enough to see with the naked eye.

● Brighter, and easier to see, are large spacecraft, such as the U.S. Space Shuttle and the Soviet *Mir*, as they circle Earth in low orbit.

● Watch for spectacular "fireworks" as debris reenters the atmosphere. The low-Earth orbit is crammed with discarded launch vehicles, satellites, and even astronauts' gloves, which eventually fall to Earth. Check the news media for predicted reentries.

TO THE MOON

OUR CLOSEST NEIGHBOR IN SPACE, the Moon, is only 384,400 km away, and a natural target for spacecraft. On September 13, 1959, the first probe—the Soviet *Luna 2*—smashed into the surface. Two years later, President Kennedy pledged that the U.S. would place a man on the Moon by the end of the 1960s, and the U.S. succeeded on July 21, 1969. Since 1972, when the U.S. stopped sending astronauts to the Moon, there have been only three Soviet lunar probes—the last in 1974. Recently, however, several nations have expressed interest in a new wave of lunar exploration and in building Moon bases where people can live and mine the rich minerals in the lunar soil.

Flying the flag: David Scott, commander of the Apollo 15 mission, salutes the flag—specially stiffened so it appears to be blowing in the nonexistent wind—outside the Lunar Module. This was the first mission on which the Lunar Roving Vehicle (right) was used.

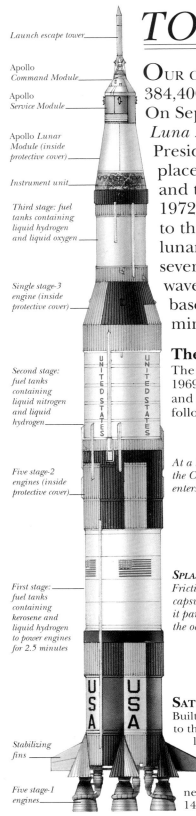

Launch escape tower

Apollo Command Module

Apollo Service Module

Apollo Lunar Module (inside protective cover)

Instrument unit

Third stage: fuel tanks containing liquid hydrogen and liquid oxygen

Single stage-3 engine (inside protective cover)

Second stage: fuel tanks containing liquid nitrogen and liquid hydrogen

Five stage-2 engines (inside protective cover)

First stage: fuel tanks containing kerosene and liquid hydrogen to power engines for 2.5 minutes

Stabilizing fins

Five stage-1 engines

UNITED STATES UNITED STATES

USA USA

The way to the Moon
The first manned mission to the Moon, *Apollo 11* in July 1969, required a complex choreography of spacecraft and orbits. Five other successful missions followed the same route.

At a height of 120 km, the Command Module enters the atmosphere.

16

SPLASHDOWN
Friction sears the capsule **17** before it parachutes into the ocean **18**.

SATURN V
Built to send astronauts to the Moon, the three-stage launch vehicle stood 111 meters high and, with fuel, weighed 2,910 tonnes (metric tons). It was capable of developing a thrust of nearly 3,500 tonnes and of putting 140 tonnes of equipment into space.

15 Approaching Earth, the Command Module with the three astronauts separates from the Service Module.

After the second-stage engines burn out **3**, the third stage fires and puts Apollo into orbit **4**.

4
3
LIFT-OFF
After launch from Cape Canaveral **1**, the first stage of the Saturn V is jettisoned **2** at a height of 60 km.

1
2
18
17

5
After orbiting 190 km above Earth, the engine on the third stage fires again to send the Apollo craft toward the Moon.

6
The Command and Service Modules separate from the third stage, allowing the protective covers around the Lunar Module to open.

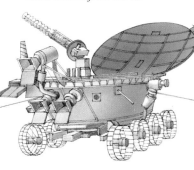

Lunar landers
Dozens of Soviet and American probes have landed on the Moon. The first to achieve a "soft landing" instead of crashing into the surface was the Soviet *Luna 9* on February 13, 1966.

LUNA 9
After bouncing across the surface, the "petals" and antennas opened, and the TV camera sent back the first pictures from the Moon's surface.

SURVEYORS
Five American Surveyor craft landed in 1966–68. They sent back more than 80,000 pictures and checked whether the lunar soil could support the Apollo Lunar Module.

LUNA 16
In 1970, this Soviet craft sent some lunar soil to Earth without any help from astronauts. It drilled out a sample and placed it in the rocket-powered capsule on top, which then blasted off back to Earth.

LUNOKHOD 1
Looking like a wheeled bathtub with a lid, the half-tonne Lunokhod traveled 10 km over the Moon's surface for several months in 1970–71. Five people controlled the Lunokhod by radio control from Earth.

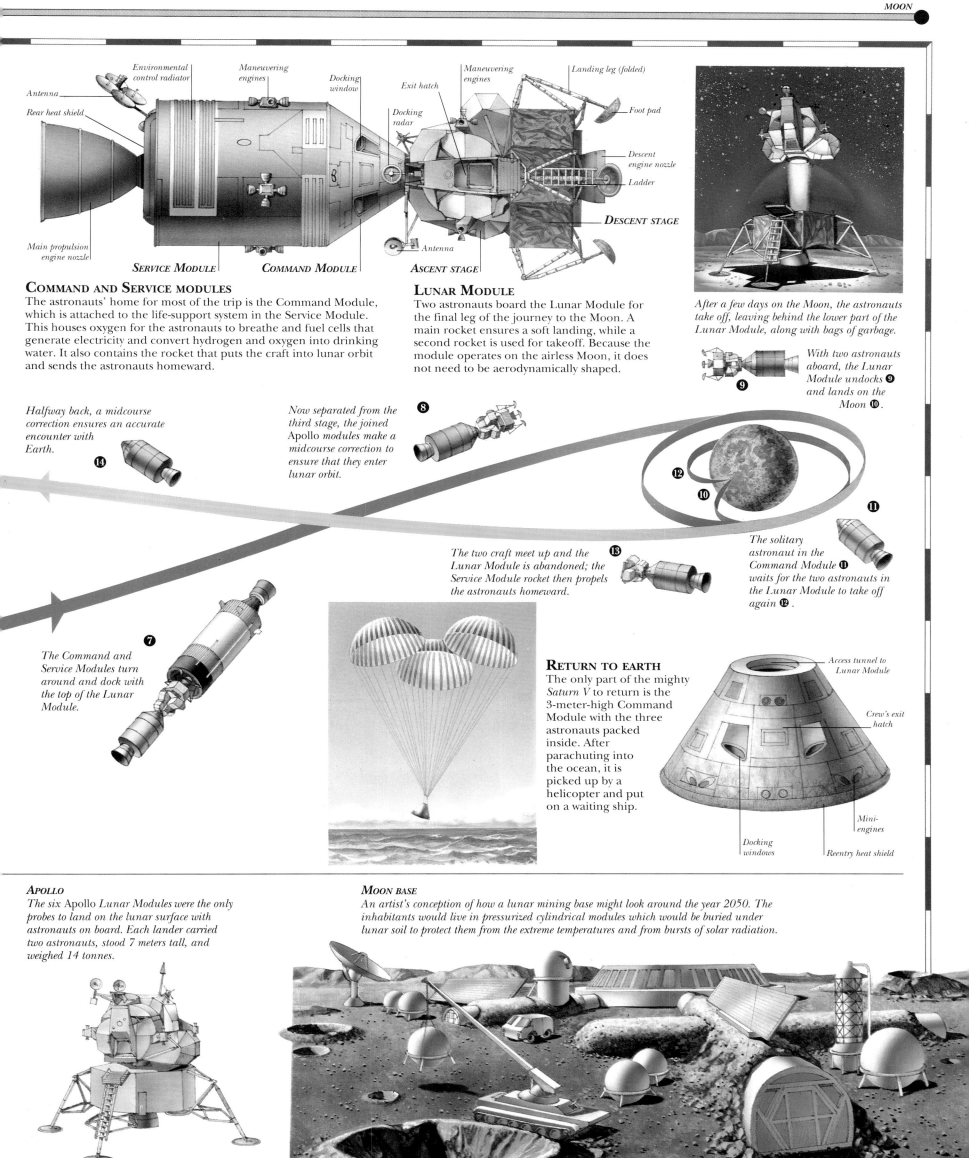

Antenna

Rear heat shield

Environmental control radiator

Maneuvering engines

Docking window

Maneuvering engines

Exit hatch

Landing leg (folded)

Docking radar

Foot pad

Descent engine nozzle

Ladder

DESCENT STAGE

Main propulsion engine nozzle

Antenna

SERVICE MODULE | **COMMAND MODULE**

ASCENT STAGE

After a few days on the Moon, the astronauts take off, leaving behind the lower part of the Lunar Module, along with bags of garbage.

COMMAND AND SERVICE MODULES

The astronauts' home for most of the trip is the Command Module, which is attached to the life-support system in the Service Module. This houses oxygen for the astronauts to breathe and fuel cells that generate electricity and convert hydrogen and oxygen into drinking water. It also contains the rocket that puts the craft into lunar orbit and sends the astronauts homeward.

LUNAR MODULE

Two astronauts board the Lunar Module for the final leg of the journey to the Moon. A main rocket ensures a soft landing, while a second rocket is used for takeoff. Because the module operates on the airless Moon, it does not need to be aerodynamically shaped.

With two astronauts aboard, the Lunar Module undocks ❾ and lands on the Moon ❿.

Halfway back, a midcourse correction ensures an accurate encounter with Earth.

❿

Now separated from the third stage, the joined Apollo modules make a midcourse correction to ensure that they enter lunar orbit.

❽

❷

❿

❶

❶

The solitary astronaut in the Command Module ❶ waits for the two astronauts in the Lunar Module to take off again ❷ .

❼

The Command and Service Modules turn around and dock with the top of the Lunar Module.

The two craft meet up and the Lunar Module is abandoned; the Service Module rocket then propels the astronauts homeward.

❸

RETURN TO EARTH

The only part of the mighty *Saturn V* to return is the 3-meter-high Command Module with the three astronauts packed inside. After parachuting into the ocean, it is picked up by a helicopter and put on a waiting ship.

Access tunnel to Lunar Module

Crew's exit hatch

Docking windows

Mini-engines

Reentry heat shield

APOLLO

The six Apollo Lunar Modules were the only probes to land on the lunar surface with astronauts on board. Each lander carried two astronauts, stood 7 meters tall, and weighed 14 tonnes.

MOON BASE

An artist's conception of how a lunar mining base might look around the year 2050. The inhabitants would live in pressurized cylindrical modules which would be buried under lunar soil to protect them from the extreme temperatures and from bursts of solar radiation.

THE MOON

EARTH'S COMPANION IN SPACE is the Moon. Some planets may have large families of moons, but each of the moons is small compared with its "parent" planet. The Moon is more than a quarter of the size of Earth, and the two act more like a "double planet." There is little in the way of family resemblance, however: Earth has an active surface that is constantly changing, large oceans, and an atmosphere that protects the planet; the Moon is a dead, barren, and airless world.

View from space: the Moon as seen by the Apollo 11 astronauts on their way home.

Earth

DOUBLE PLANET   5.1°
The Moon is large compared to Earth: only Charon, Pluto's moon, is bigger in comparison to its "parent." The Moon's equator is tilted by 5.1° from Earth's orbit around the Sun. It spins around in 27.3 days—the same time as it takes to orbit Earth.

PRESERVED CRATERS
Between 4.6 and 3.5 billion years ago—in the early years of the Solar System—thousands of meteorites bombarded the Moon. The surface is littered with craters, most of which are perfectly preserved: the Moon has no atmosphere, volcanoes, or earthquakes that would change the appearance of the surface.

MARE IMBRIUM
This dark plain (one of the so-called seas or maria) was once a crater about 1,000 km wide. It was formed nearly 4 billion years ago, but molten rock, or lava, seeped out through the Moon's surface and filled the crater.

DARK PLATO
This is one of a handful of craters with a dark floor. As with the maria, lava seeped out from the Moon after the impact and solidified into a dark rock.

MARE SERENITATIS
The maria have romantic names: Serenitatis is Latin for Serenity, while Mare Nectaris means Sea of Nectar. Sinus Iridum is the Bay of Rainbows, and Oceanus Procellarum is the Ocean of Storms.

MONTES HAEMUS
Mountain ranges like Haemus are really the walls of enormous craters, the maria. The peaks in the Haemus are thousands of meters high.

NEWCOMERS
Ray craters are recent arrivals on the lunar scene. Copernicus, one of the most conspicuous, is about 800 million years old. The "rays" are fragments of bright rock splashed out by the impact.

LUNAR HIGHLANDS
The areas between the maria, the lunar highlands, are rougher, brighter, and older than the maria, or lowlands.

CRATER NAMESAKES
The craters on the near side are named after famous historical figures, many of whom were important astronomers.

The near side
The Moon spins on its axis in exactly the time that it takes to complete an orbit of Earth. This is because the strong pull from Earth's gravity has gradually "braked" the Moon's spin, which originally was faster. As a result, the same side of the Moon—the near side—always faces Earth. Astronomers have extensively mapped the near side from both Earth and space, and all the lunar landings have been on this side. The dark areas, which early astronomers thought to be seas, make up the familiar features of "the man in the Moon."

Map labels: Herschel, Pythagoras, MARE FRIGORIS, De La Rue, Plato, Alpes Montes, Aristoteles, Atlas, Hercules, Eudoxus, Cassini, Montes Caucasus, Posidonius, Cleomedes, Aristillus, Archimedes, MARE SERENITATIS, Montes Apenninus, Montes Haemus, Aristarchus, MARE IMBRIUM, SINUS RORIS, Montes Jura, SINUS IRIDUM, Eratosthenes, VAPORUM, Julius Caesar, MARE TRANQUILLITATIS, Montes Carpatus, Stadius, Copernicus, Taruntius, OCEANUS PROCELLARUM, Kepler, Landsberg, Hipparchus, Délambre, MARE FECUNDITATIS, Langrenus, Encke, Hevelius, Flamsteed, Fra Mauro, Ptolemaeus, Albategnius, Theophilus, Cyrillus, Vendelinus, Grimaldi, MARE NUBIUM, Alphonsus, Arzachel, MARE NECTARIS, Letronne, Mersenius, Gassendi, Bullialdus, Krusenstern, Purbach, Fracastorius, Petavius, Humboldt, MARE HUMORUM, Pitatus, Walter, Furnerius, Hörbinger, Piccolomini, Janssen, Wilhelm, Stöfler, Maurolycus, Schickard, Tycho, Longomontanus, Maginus, Schiller, Clavius, Bailly

LANDING SITES
The map shows the landing sites of 15 robot explorers—the Soviet *Luna*, and the U.S. *Surveyor* and *Ranger* probes—as well as the 12 *Apollo* astronauts.

7 *Ranger* (Mission numbers: 7, 8, & 9)

9 *Luna* (Mission numbers: 9, 13, 16, 17, 20, 21, & 24)

A *Surveyor* (Mission numbers: 1, 3, 5, 6, & 7)

11 *Apollo* (Mission numbers: 11, 12, 14, 15, 16, & 17)

RADIUS: 1,738 KILOMETERS

STRUCTURE

CRUST

MANTLE

PARTIALLY MOLTEN ZONE

CORE

INSIDE THE MOON
The solid crust is made of a rock much like granite. Below the crust is the mantle, consisting of a darker rock. Deeper still is a partly molten region where "moonquakes" occur. The core may be made of iron, but scientists cannot be certain yet.

FACTS AND FIGURES

Diameter	3,476 km
Average distance from Earth	384,400 km
Orbital speed around Earth	1.02 km/sec
Circles Earth (a month)	27.3 days
A day:	
Turns on axis	27.3 days
New moon to new moon	29.5 days
Mass (Earth = 1)	0.012
Average density (water = 1)	3.34
Surface gravity (Earth = 1)	0.16
Surface temperature	−155°C to 105°C

ACTIVITIES

● With the naked eye you can see the largest maria, and the ray craters Tycho and Copernicus.

● Binoculars reveal surprising detail. Use the near-side map to see how many features you can spot.

● With a small telescope you will find that some features will more than fill the telescope's field of view.

● Sketch craters to practice observing techniques. You will see more detail when the Moon is illuminated from the side than when it is full.

SOVIET INFLUENCE
The craters on the far side are named after scientists and philosophers, especially Soviet ones.

AN AIRLESS VIEW
The lack of an atmosphere on the Moon has given the lunar orbiters exceptionally clear views of the surface. Without a blanket of air, however, surface temperatures soar to 105°C during the day and drop to −155°C at night.

MARE MOSCOVIENSE
This is one of the few maria on the far side. The crust is thicker on this side, making it more difficult for lava to seep through into the basins. But why the crust should be thicker is a mystery in itself.

SCREENED FROM EARTH
The airless conditions make the Moon an ideal place for an observatory, especially on the far side. Optical and radio astronomers working here would be screened from all the stray light and electrical signals that radiate from Earth.

TSIOLKOVSKY
A dark floor makes this crater stand out. There is also an impressive mountain range within this 180-km-wide crater.

The far side
Until October 1959 no one had seen the Moon's far side—the part that always faces away from Earth. Then a Soviet probe, *Luna 3*, swung behind the Moon and sent back pictures of the far side. The pictures ended speculation that the gravity of the Moon might be stronger on that side, making an atmosphere and even inhabitants a possibility. Instead, the far side is even more heavily cratered than the near side, but with far fewer "seas." Why this should be is a mystery.

MARE ORIENTALE
This 900-km-wide basin is one of the most spectacular lunar features. A huge meteorite hit the surface, and the shock threw up the mountains that surround the crater.

MOUNTAIN RINGS
The rings of mountains around Mare Orientale were discovered from Earth. We can see a little of the far side from Earth, because the Moon "swings" slightly in its orbit (see page 17).

SOUTHERN MYSTERY
Not all the Moon is mapped. There is a tiny area around the south pole which has yet to be explored.

GALILEO'S IMPACT
The Galileo space probe turned its cameras on the Moon as it swung around Earth on its way to Jupiter in 1990. The probe found that the craters in this region have largely destroyed a very old, and very large, impact basin.

Crater and mare labels on the map:
Schwarzschild, Compton, Avogadro, Somerfeld, Stebbins, Rowland, Birkhoff, Fabry, D'Alembert, Campbell, Von Neumann, Wiener, Szilard, Shajn, Fowler, Landau, Joliot, Seyfert, MARE MOSCOVIENSE, Trumpler, Charlier, Fleming, Buys Ballot, Cockcroft, Joule, Guyot, Ostwald, Poynting, Mach, Kekule, Mendeleev, Papaleski, Schuster, Mandelstam, Fersman, Chaplygin, Tsander, Michelson, Keeler, Heaviside, Korolev, Hertzsprung, Gagarin, Langemak, Aitken, Doppler, Galois, Pasteur, Van de Graaf, Hilbert, Leeuwenhoek, Oppenheimer, Chebyshev, Tsiolkovsky, Pavlov, Leibnitz, Apollo, Milne, Jules Verne, Von Karman, Roche, Mendel, Planck, Poincare, Minkowski, Rima Planck, MARE AUSTRALE, Schrödinger, Lemaitre, Zeeman, Antoniadi, Montes Cordillera, Montes Rook, MARE ORIENTALE, MARE SMYTHII

EARTH'S SATELLITE

THE MOON ACCOMPANIES EARTH as it moves around the Sun, orbiting our planet like a large artificial satellite. Each night, the shape of the Moon seems to change. These "changes"—the Moon's phases—occur because our view of the sunlit part of the Moon alters as it circles Earth. Once or twice a year, the Moon moves into Earth's shadow, and our planet eclipses the Moon by blocking off the sunlight. A rarer but more spectacular sight is when the Moon's shadow falls on our planet and day is turned into night. Phases and eclipses, however, are no mystery to modern space scientists. The challenge they face is finding out where the Moon came from and how it has changed in its 4.6 billion-year history.

Total eclipse: the Moon completely covers the Sun's disk, giving us a glimpse of the Sun's outer atmosphere, the corona.

ECLIPSE OF THE SUN

By coincidence, the Moon and Sun appear to be the same size in our sky. Sometimes at New Moon, the Moon's shadow falls on Earth. People in the small area where the inner shadow falls see a total eclipse. Those under the outer area see just part of the Sun eclipsed.

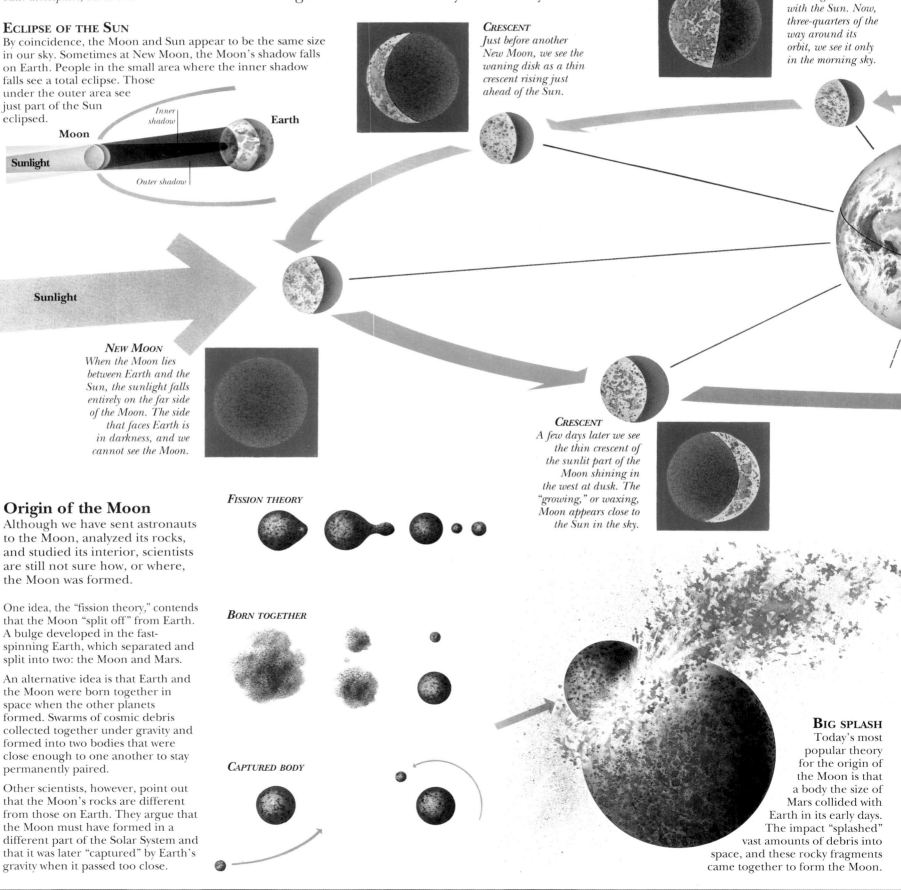

Moon *Inner shadow* *Earth*

Sunlight

Outer shadow

Sunlight

CRESCENT
Just before another New Moon, we see the waning disk as a thin crescent rising just ahead of the Sun.

LAST QUARTER
The Moon is drawing back in line with the Sun. Now, three-quarters of the way around its orbit, we see it only in the morning sky.

NEW MOON
When the Moon lies between Earth and the Sun, the sunlight falls entirely on the far side of the Moon. The side that faces Earth is in darkness, and we cannot see the Moon.

CRESCENT
A few days later we see the thin crescent of the sunlit part of the Moon shining in the west at dusk. The "growing," or waxing, Moon appears close to the Sun in the sky.

Origin of the Moon

Although we have sent astronauts to the Moon, analyzed its rocks, and studied its interior, scientists are still not sure how, or where, the Moon was formed.

One idea, the "fission theory," contends that the Moon "split off" from Earth. A bulge developed in the fast-spinning Earth, which separated and split into two: the Moon and Mars.

An alternative idea is that Earth and the Moon were born together in space when the other planets formed. Swarms of cosmic debris collected together under gravity and formed into two bodies that were close enough to one another to stay permanently paired.

Other scientists, however, point out that the Moon's rocks are different from those on Earth. They argue that the Moon must have formed in a different part of the Solar System and that it was later "captured" by Earth's gravity when it passed too close.

FISSION THEORY

BORN TOGETHER

CAPTURED BODY

BIG SPLASH
Today's most popular theory for the origin of the Moon is that a body the size of Mars collided with Earth in its early days. The impact "splashed" vast amounts of debris into space, and these rocky fragments came together to form the Moon.

Seeing around the edge

The Moon's orbit around our planet is not quite circular: it varies between 363,000 and 406,000 km from the center of Earth. As a result, the Moon's speed changes during the orbit: it goes faster when close to Earth and slower when farther away. This means that the Moon sometimes surges ahead or lags behind Earth. When this happens, we can peek around the Moon's edge. This effect, called libration, allows us to see 59% of the Moon's surface, rather than just half.

The Moon spins on its axis at a constant rate, but its speed around its slightly oval orbit changes.

The Moon has lagged behind Earth; now we can see around the opposite edge.

Earth

Near side

At the nearest point, we cannot see any of the far side.

Far side

Farthest from Earth: all of the far side is again hidden.

The Moon has surged ahead of Earth on its orbit, and we see part of its far side.

Disappearing trick: a partial eclipse as the upper left side of the Moon enters the darkest part of the shadow cast by Earth.

GIBBOUS
The Moon has now started to "shrink" or wane. A few days after Full Moon, part of the sunlit side has disappeared from our view.

Outer shadow

Earth

Sunlight

Moon

Inner shadow

ECLIPSE OF THE MOON
A lunar eclipse takes place when the Moon moves into Earth's shadow. Most months, the Moon passes above or below the shadow because its orbit is tilted by 5° from Earth's path around the Sun. Only when it crosses Earth's orbit at Full Moon is there a lunar eclipse.

FULL MOON
When the Moon is directly behind Earth (but not in its shadow), sunlight illuminates all of the near side of the Moon. We now see a Full Moon.

GIBBOUS
Three or four days later, the sunlight illuminates nearly all of the near side—a "bulging" phase that is called gibbous.

FIRST QUARTER
The Moon is now a quarter of the way around its orbit. From Earth we see half the Moon illuminated.

E C L I P S E S

Over the next few years, there will be several total eclipses of the Sun and Moon.

Lunar	Visible from
Dec. 9–10, 1992	Asia, Europe, Central America
June 4, 1993	Australasia, Pacific Ocean, Antarctica
Nov. 29, 1993	Europe, the Americas, North Asia
Apr. 3–4, 1996	Africa, Europe, S. America
Sep. 27, 1996	W. Africa, Europe, the Americas
Sep. 16, 1997	Australasia, Africa, Europe
Jan. 21, 2000	Asia, the Americas, Europe

Solar	Visible from
June 30, 1992	S. America, W. and S.W. Africa
Nov. 3, 1994	Central and S. America, S. Africa
Oct. 24, 1995	Asia, Australia, Japan, S. America
Mar. 8–9, 1997	Japan, Philippines, N.W. America
Feb. 26, 1998	Hawaii, America, W. Africa
Aug. 11, 1999	Greenland, Europe, N. Africa, Arabia

History of the Moon
The Moon has suffered a history of bombardment from space. With no air, water, or volcanoes to erode the evidence, it is an impact-scarred little world.

2.8 BILLION YEARS AGO
Bombardment has nearly ceased: there are very few fresh craters. The appearance, however, is transformed by dark basaltic lava, which seeped through the surface to fill the deep maria basins.

TODAY
The Moon has changed very little in the past 2.8 billion years. The only new features are a few youthful impact craters, such as Copernicus, with their bright ray systems.

3.8 BILLION YEARS AGO
The crust is completely covered with craters of all sizes. The huge scar at top left is the young Mare Imbrium, looking like today's Mare Orientale.

THE SOLAR SYSTEM

OUR NEIGHBORHOOD IN SPACE consists of our local star, the Sun, and its family of nine planets, nearly 70 moons, millions of comets, and countless asteroids. For most of the time, Pluto is the outermost planet, circling the Sun at an average distance of 6 billion kilometers. The nearest star, however, is nearly 7,000 times farther away—which shows just how small our neighborhood is. Dominating the entire Solar System is the Sun, which is nearly a thousand times more massive than all the planets put together. The energy the Sun generates by nuclear fusion makes it luminous and provides the rest of the Solar System with heat and light. Its gravity pulls the planets so that they move around it in almost circular orbits. The nine planets fall into two groups: four small rocky ones close to the Sun and four big gassy ones farther out (Pluto is a puzzle as it does not fit into either group). Each planet, however, has its own distinct characteristics.

PLUTO
Pluto's highly elliptical orbit sometimes brings it inside Neptune's orbit so that, between 1979 and 1999, Neptune takes its place as the most distant planet from the Sun. Pluto is the smallest planet by far, and its moon, Charon, is fully half its size.

URANUS
This planet circles the Sun on its side. Compared with the other gas giants, Uranus is a bland, serene planet. It has 11 rings and 15 moons, some of which have bizarre surface features.

NEPTUNE
Of the four worlds made almost entirely of gas—the gas giants—Neptune is farthest from the Sun. It has enormous storms and the fastest winds in the Solar System. It also has four rings and eight moons.

Orbit of Halley's Comet

HALLEY'S COMET
An elongated orbit carries this small lump of cosmic debris out as far as Neptune and as close in as Venus. Halley's Comet is the most famous of the millions of comets that orbit the Sun.

Planet	Diameter (equatorial)	Average distance from Sun	Orbital speed around Sun	Circles Sun (a "year")	Maximum magnitude in sky	Number of known moons
Mercury	4,878 km	57,910,000 km	47.89 km/sec	87.97 days	−1.4	0
Venus	12,103 km	108,200,000 km	35.03 km/sec	224.70 days	−4.4	0
Earth	12,756 km	149,600,000 km	29.79 km/sec	365.26 days		1
Mars	6,786 km	227,940,000 km	24.13 km/sec	686.98 days	−2.8	2
Jupiter	142,984 km	778,330,000 km	13.06 km/sec	11.86 years	−2.8	16
Saturn	120,536 km	1,426,980,000 km	9.64 km/sec	29.46 years	−0.3	18
Uranus	51,118 km	2,870,990,000 km	6.81 km/sec	84.01 years	+5.5	15
Neptune	49,528 km	4,497,070,000 km	5.43 km/sec	164.79 years	+7.8	8
Pluto	2,284 km	5,913,520,000 km	4.74 km/sec	248.54 years	+13.6	1

HOW FAR FROM THE SUN?
The scale below shows the average distance at which the planets orbit the Sun.

Pluto

Neptune

Pluto (at its farthest) 49.3 AU

Pluto's average distance from the Sun is 5,914 million km, but it has a very elongated orbit, which takes it as far out as 7,380 million km from the Sun and as close in as 4,430 million km.

Neptune 30.1 AU   Pluto (at its closest) 29.6 AU

49 48 47 46 45 44 43 42 41 40 39 38 37 36 35 34 33 32 31   29 28 27

Astronomical units: A useful yardstick for comparing distances in the Solar System is the astronomical unit (AU)—the average distance between Earth and the Sun.

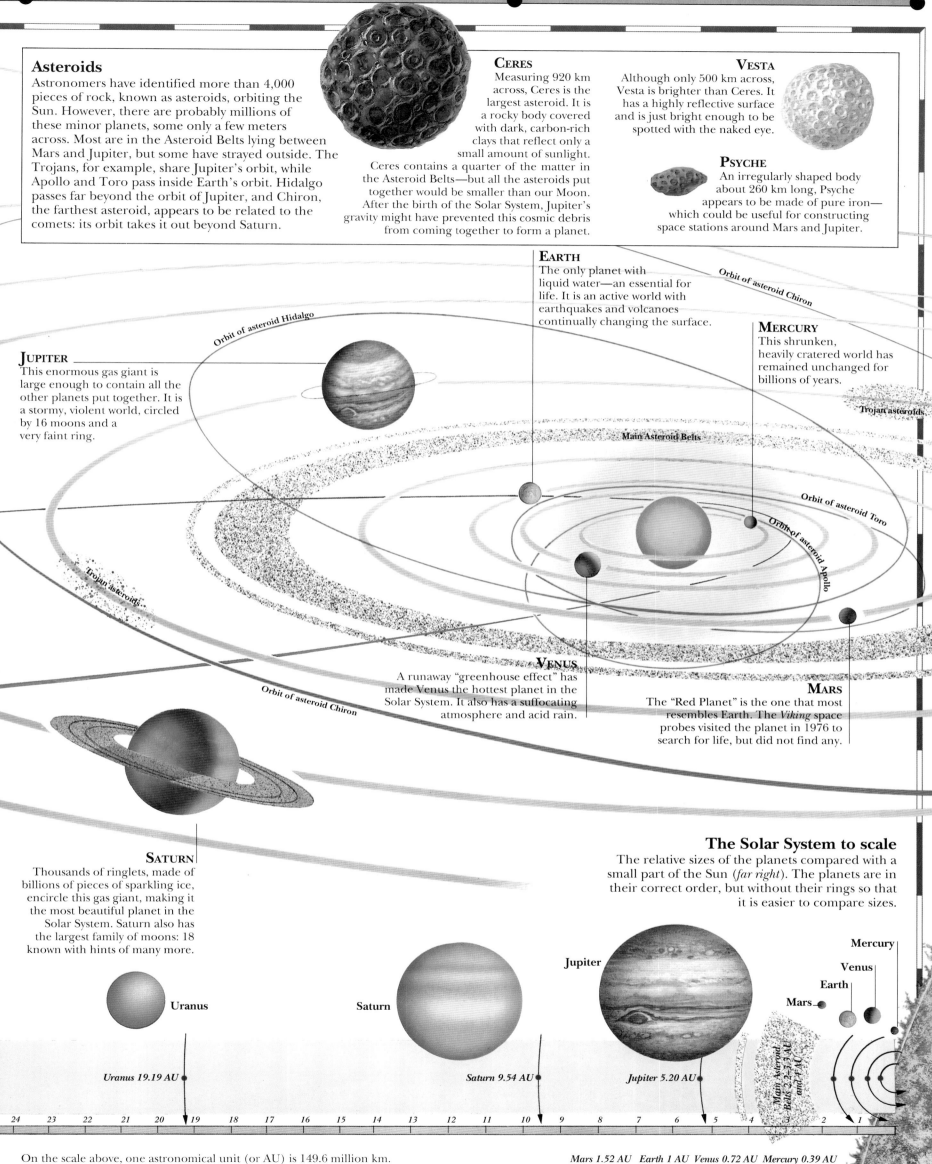

Asteroids

Astronomers have identified more than 4,000 pieces of rock, known as asteroids, orbiting the Sun. However, there are probably millions of these minor planets, some only a few meters across. Most are in the Asteroid Belts lying between Mars and Jupiter, but some have strayed outside. The Trojans, for example, share Jupiter's orbit, while Apollo and Toro pass inside Earth's orbit. Hidalgo passes far beyond the orbit of Jupiter, and Chiron, the farthest asteroid, appears to be related to the comets: its orbit takes it out beyond Saturn.

CERES

Measuring 920 km across, Ceres is the largest asteroid. It is a rocky body covered with dark, carbon-rich clays that reflect only a small amount of sunlight. Ceres contains a quarter of the matter in the Asteroid Belts—but all the asteroids put together would be smaller than our Moon. After the birth of the Solar System, Jupiter's gravity might have prevented this cosmic debris from coming together to form a planet.

VESTA

Although only 500 km across, Vesta is brighter than Ceres. It has a highly reflective surface and is just bright enough to be spotted with the naked eye.

PSYCHE

An irregularly shaped body about 260 km long, Psyche appears to be made of pure iron—which could be useful for constructing space stations around Mars and Jupiter.

EARTH

The only planet with liquid water—an essential for life. It is an active world with earthquakes and volcanoes continually changing the surface.

MERCURY

This shrunken, heavily cratered world has remained unchanged for billions of years.

JUPITER

This enormous gas giant is large enough to contain all the other planets put together. It is a stormy, violent world, circled by 16 moons and a very faint ring.

Orbit of asteroid Chiron

Orbit of asteroid Hidalgo

Trojan asteroids

Main Asteroid Belts

Orbit of asteroid Toro

Orbit of asteroid Apollo

Trojan asteroids

Orbit of asteroid Chiron

VENUS

A runaway "greenhouse effect" has made Venus the hottest planet in the Solar System. It also has a suffocating atmosphere and acid rain.

MARS

The "Red Planet" is the one that most resembles Earth. The *Viking* space probes visited the planet in 1976 to search for life, but did not find any.

SATURN

Thousands of ringlets, made of billions of pieces of sparkling ice, encircle this gas giant, making it the most beautiful planet in the Solar System. Saturn also has the largest family of moons: 18 known with hints of many more.

The Solar System to scale

The relative sizes of the planets compared with a small part of the Sun (*far right*). The planets are in their correct order, but without their rings so that it is easier to compare sizes.

Uranus

Saturn

Jupiter

Mercury

Venus

Earth

Mars

Main Asteroid Belts 2.2–3.3 AU

Uranus 19.19 AU   *Saturn 9.54 AU*   *Jupiter 5.20 AU*

| 24 | 23 | 22 | 21 | 20 | 19 | 18 | 17 | 16 | 15 | 14 | 13 | 12 | 11 | 10 | 9 | 8 | 7 | 6 | 5 | 4 | 3 | 2 | 1 |

On the scale above, one astronomical unit (or AU) is 149.6 million km.

Mars 1.52 AU   Earth 1 AU   Venus 0.72 AU   Mercury 0.39 AU

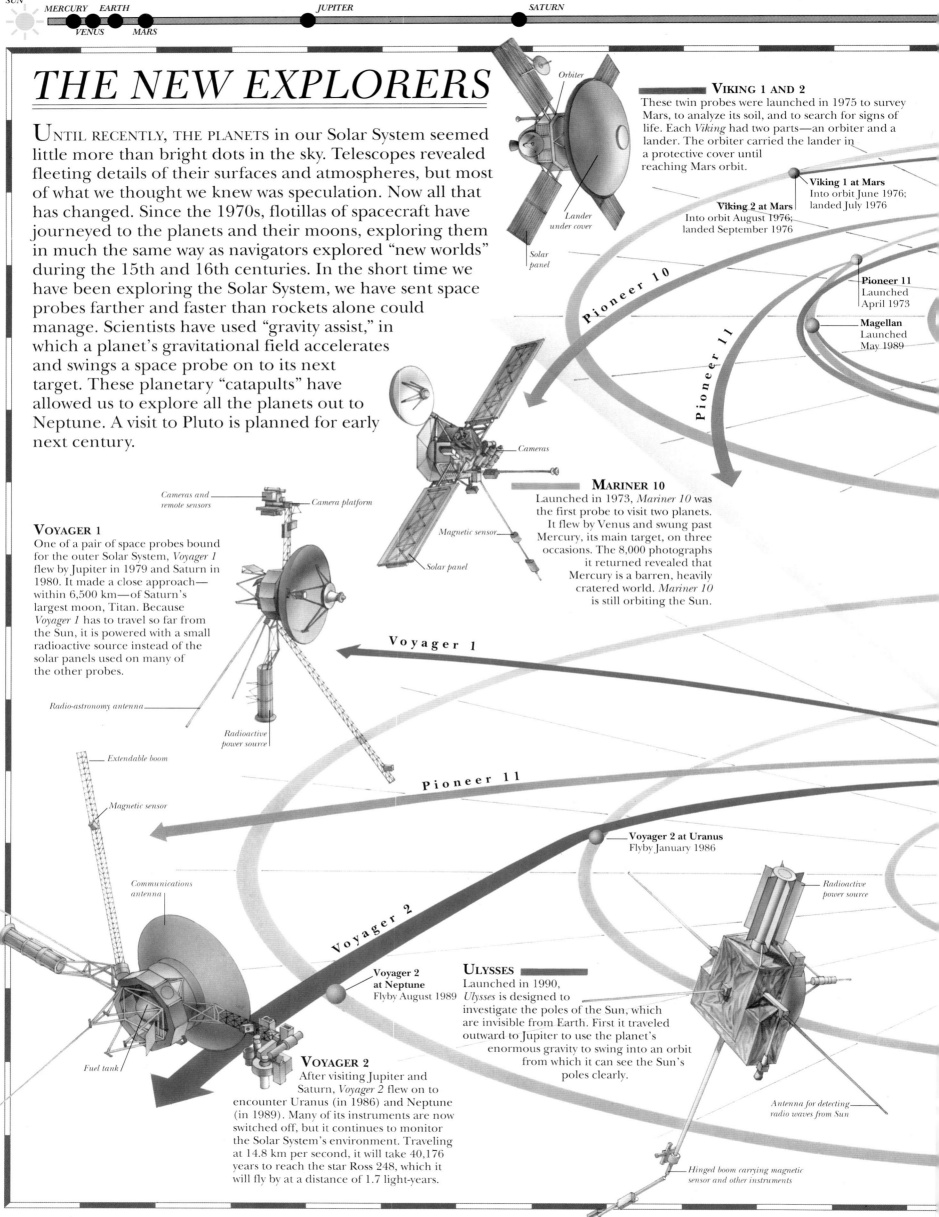

THE NEW EXPLORERS

Until recently, the planets in our Solar System seemed little more than bright dots in the sky. Telescopes revealed fleeting details of their surfaces and atmospheres, but most of what we thought we knew was speculation. Now all that has changed. Since the 1970s, flotillas of spacecraft have journeyed to the planets and their moons, exploring them in much the same way as navigators explored "new worlds" during the 15th and 16th centuries. In the short time we have been exploring the Solar System, we have sent space probes farther and faster than rockets alone could manage. Scientists have used "gravity assist," in which a planet's gravitational field accelerates and swings a space probe on to its next target. These planetary "catapults" have allowed us to explore all the planets out to Neptune. A visit to Pluto is planned for early next century.

VIKING 1 AND 2
These twin probes were launched in 1975 to survey Mars, to analyze its soil, and to search for signs of life. Each *Viking* had two parts—an orbiter and a lander. The orbiter carried the lander in a protective cover until reaching Mars orbit.

Orbiter

Lander under cover

Solar panel

Viking 1 at Mars
Into orbit June 1976; landed July 1976

Viking 2 at Mars
Into orbit August 1976; landed September 1976

Pioneer 11
Launched April 1973

Magellan
Launched May 1989

Pioneer 10

Pioneer 11

VOYAGER 1
One of a pair of space probes bound for the outer Solar System, *Voyager 1* flew by Jupiter in 1979 and Saturn in 1980. It made a close approach—within 6,500 km—of Saturn's largest moon, Titan. Because *Voyager 1* has to travel so far from the Sun, it is powered with a small radioactive source instead of the solar panels used on many of the other probes.

Cameras and remote sensors

Camera platform

Cameras

Magnetic sensor

Solar panel

MARINER 10
Launched in 1973, *Mariner 10* was the first probe to visit two planets. It flew by Venus and swung past Mercury, its main target, on three occasions. The 8,000 photographs it returned revealed that Mercury is a barren, heavily cratered world. *Mariner 10* is still orbiting the Sun.

Radio-astronomy antenna

Radioactive power source

Voyager 1

Extendable boom

Magnetic sensor

Pioneer 11

Voyager 2 at Uranus
Flyby January 1986

Communications antenna

Voyager 2

Voyager 2 at Neptune
Flyby August 1989

ULYSSES
Launched in 1990, *Ulysses* is designed to investigate the poles of the Sun, which are invisible from Earth. First it traveled outward to Jupiter to use the planet's enormous gravity to swing into an orbit from which it can see the Sun's poles clearly.

Radioactive power source

VOYAGER 2
After visiting Jupiter and Saturn, *Voyager 2* flew on to encounter Uranus (in 1986) and Neptune (in 1989). Many of its instruments are now switched off, but it continues to monitor the Solar System's environment. Traveling at 14.8 km per second, it will take 40,176 years to reach the star Ross 248, which it will fly by at a distance of 1.7 light-years.

Fuel tank

Antenna for detecting radio waves from Sun

Hinged boom carrying magnetic sensor and other instruments

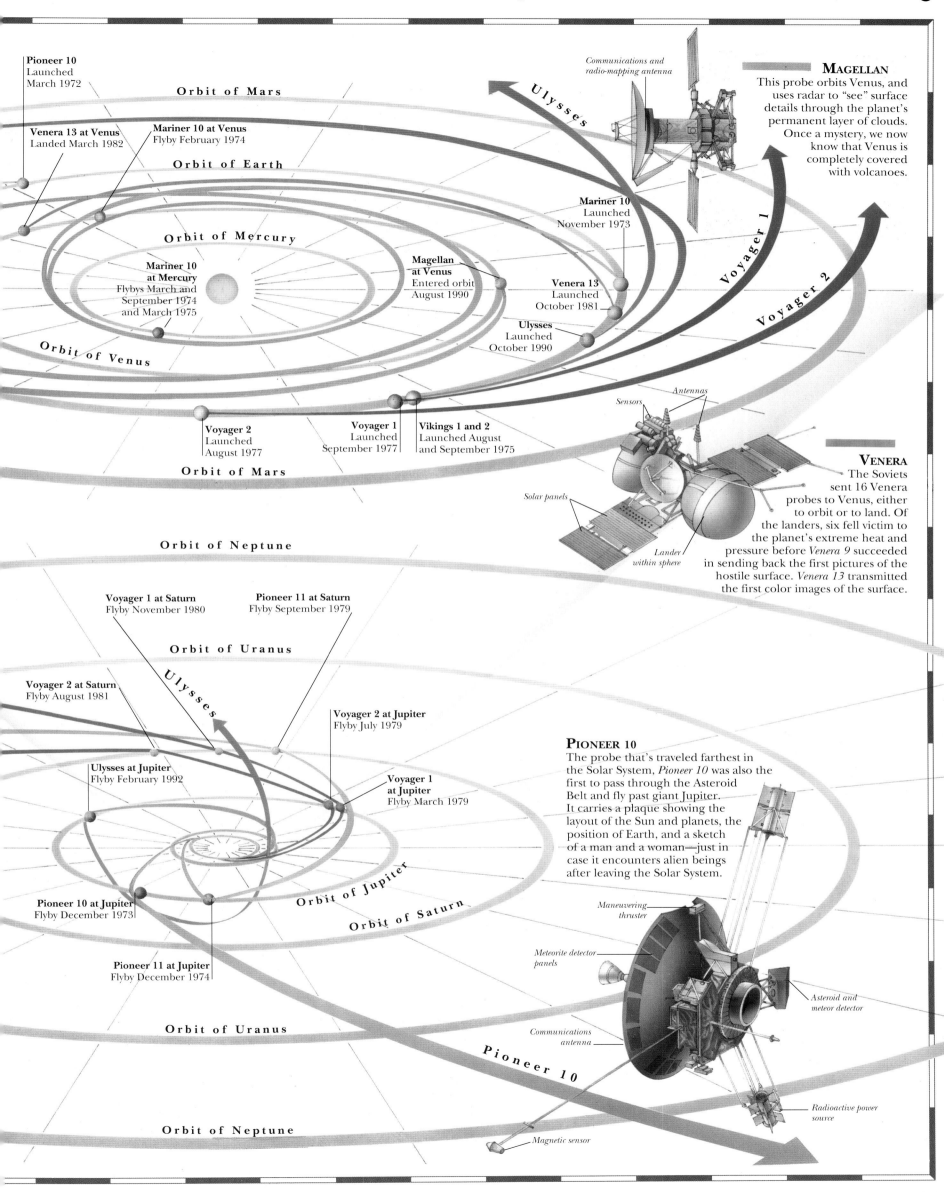

Pioneer 10
Launched
March 1972

Venera 13 at Venus
Landed March 1982

Mariner 10 at Venus
Flyby February 1974

Orbit of Mars

Orbit of Earth

Orbit of Mercury

**Mariner 10
at Mercury**
Flybys March and
September 1974
and March 1975

Orbit of Venus

**Magellan
at Venus**
Entered orbit
August 1990

Voyager 2
Launched
August 1977

Voyager 1
Launched
September 1977

Vikings 1 and 2
Launched August
and September 1975

Orbit of Mars

Mariner 10
Launched
November 1973

Venera 13
Launched
October 1981

Ulysses
Launched
October 1990

Communications and
radio-mapping antenna

Ulysses

Voyager 1

Voyager 2

MAGELLAN
This probe orbits Venus, and
uses radar to "see" surface
details through the planet's
permanent layer of clouds.
Once a mystery, we now
know that Venus is
completely covered
with volcanoes.

Antennas

Sensors

Solar panels

Lander
within sphere

VENERA
The Soviets
sent 16 Venera
probes to Venus, either
to orbit or to land. Of
the landers, six fell victim to
the planet's extreme heat and
pressure before *Venera 9* succeeded
in sending back the first pictures of the
hostile surface. *Venera 13* transmitted
the first color images of the surface.

Orbit of Neptune

Voyager 1 at Saturn
Flyby November 1980

Pioneer 11 at Saturn
Flyby September 1979

Orbit of Uranus

Voyager 2 at Saturn
Flyby August 1981

Ulysses

Ulysses at Jupiter
Flyby February 1992

Voyager 2 at Jupiter
Flyby July 1979

**Voyager 1
at Jupiter**
Flyby March 1979

Pioneer 10 at Jupiter
Flyby December 1973

Pioneer 11 at Jupiter
Flyby December 1974

Orbit of Jupiter

Orbit of Saturn

Orbit of Uranus

Pioneer 10

Orbit of Neptune

PIONEER 10
The probe that's traveled farthest in
the Solar System, *Pioneer 10* was also the
first to pass through the Asteroid
Belt and fly past giant Jupiter.
It carries a plaque showing the
layout of the Sun and planets, the
position of Earth, and a sketch
of a man and a woman—just in
case it encounters alien beings
after leaving the Solar System.

Maneuvering
thruster

Meteorite detector
panels

Asteroid and
meteor detector

Communications
antenna

Radioactive power
source

Magnetic sensor

MERCURY

MOST PEOPLE, EVEN SOME ASTRONOMERS, have lived their whole lives without seeing Mercury. The reason is not that Mercury is particularly faint but that, as the closest planet to the Sun, it is never far from the Sun's glare. You can glimpse it only at twilight, either just after sunset or immediately before sunrise. Mercury feels the Sun's powerful gravity very strongly and orbits at a breakneck speed—which makes it even more difficult to spot. And when you do find the planet with a telescope, it is a disappointing sight. Mercury is the second smallest of the planets and its tiny disk shows almost no detail. Only one space probe—*Mariner 10*—has been to Mercury. It photographed a barren, cratered, and shrunken world that looks remarkably like our Moon.

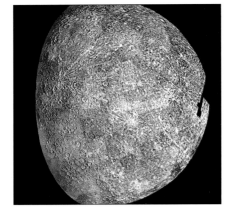

A crater-scarred surface, photographed by Mariner 10 from a distance of 48,000 km.

STRUCTURE

CRUST

MANTLE

CORE

RADIUS: 2,439 KILOMETERS

INSIDE MERCURY
A huge core of iron and nickel is covered by a rocky mantle and crust. Above this is a very thin atmosphere—a quadrillionth of Earth's. The main gases present are helium and sodium.

ATMOSPHERE

HELIUM

OTHER

OXYGEN

SODIUM

UPRIGHT PLANET
As Mercury races round the Sun, it spins on its axis so slowly that it takes 58 days 16 hours to complete one turn. But it is the most upright of the planets—its axis is tilted by just 2° from the vertical.

Earth

2°

CALORIS BASIN
The colossal crater—1,300 km across—is the scar left after a huge object, about a hundred kilometers across, collided with Mercury.

CALORIS MONTES
Outermost of several rings of mountains up to 2 km high thrown up by the Caloris impact.

North

Mercury

Magnetic field lines

South

Magnetic to the core
Scientists were surprised when *Mariner 10* found that Mercury has a magnetic field, even though it is a hundred times weaker than the one on Earth. In Earth's case, the field is thought to be caused by the rapid rate of rotation generating electric currents in the iron core (like a dynamo—*see right*). Mercury has a slow rate of spin, which should not generate electric currents, so its magnetism is evidence of a huge iron core inside the planet.

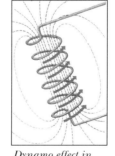

Dynamo effect in rotating planet

A day longer than a year
On Mercury, birthdays are more frequent than sunrises! The "year" (one orbit of the Sun) lasts almost 88 Earth-days. One complete "day" (sunrise to sunrise) is 176 Earth-days, or two "Mercury years." Suppose you were to stand, at sunrise, at the place marked by the black spot (position **1**). The planet, as it travels around the Sun, will be slowly spinning. For your spot, position **2** will be midmorning; **3** noon; and **4** afternoon. The Sun will set at **5**; the planet has completed one orbit, but has rotated on its axis just 1 1/2 times. On the second orbit (shown here separated) the spot will be in darkness at **6**, **7**, and **8**. At **1** the sun rises again. It is one day since the previous sunrise, but you are two years older.

4

8

1   5

7   3

6

2

THREE ROTATIONS A DAY
As shown by the black spot, Mercury has turned three times on its axis in the time it has taken to travel around the Sun twice and return to position **1**. So the "rotation period" (58 days 16 hours on Earth) is one-third the length of the "solar day" (sunrise to sunrise). Mercury's path around the Sun is also not circular: at its closest the planet comes within 46 million km of the Sun, and at its most distant strays to 70 million km.

Verdi
Turgenev
Zola
Strindberg
Mansur
Nervo
Van Eyck
Bronte
Heine
Couperin
Harunobu
Mickiewicz
Phidias
Balzac
Wang Meng
Mozart
Tyagaraja
Zeami
Theophanes
Philoxenus
Goya
Sophocles
Tolstoj
Bello
Valmiki
Beethoven
Milton
Bartok
Sayat-Nova
Ustad Isa
Liang K'ai
Surikov
Takayoshi
Michelangelo
Yakovlev
Sheller
Hawthorne
Wagner
Bach
Keats
Dickens
Cervantes
Bernini

BOREALIS PLANITIA
SUISEI PLANITIA
CALORIS BASIN
ODIN PLANITIA
SOBKOU PLANITIA
BUDH PLANITIA
TIR PLANITIA
CALORIS MONTES

Mutilated world

Mercury has a crater-scarred surface because of the intense bombardment it received early in the history of the Solar System—about 4 billion years ago. Debris remaining after the formation of the planets collided with Mercury, covering it with craters. As the bombardment continued, the planet started to shrink, so that its "skin" is now literally too big for it. Mercury has remained almost unchanged since then—a fossilized world.

Uncharted terrain: the only part that Mariner 10 was unable to see. The artist has used his imagination to draw what might be there.

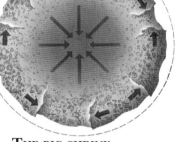

THE BIG SHRINK

Mercury is dominated by its huge iron core. As the planet cooled after being formed, the core shrank by up to 4 km. The surface buckled, resulting in long "wrinkle ridges"—some several kilometers high—that cross the cratered terrain.

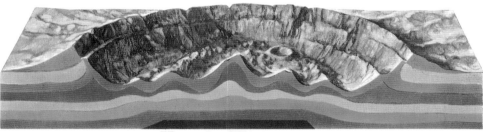

Discovery Rupes, a 400-km "wrinkle ridge," runs across ancient craters in the southern hemisphere, at a longitude of about 38° W.

West	44°	40°	36°	32°	28°	24°	20°	East

AFRICANUS HORTON

TINTORETTO   SOTATSU

DISCOVERY RUPES

SHEVCHENKO

RAMEAU

KUROSAWA

HESIOD

North   51°   53°   55°   South

POCKMARKED PLANET

Mercury still bears the scars from the myriad objects that bombarded it 4 billion years ago. Small impacts left simple, bowl-shaped craters a few kilometers across. Bigger impacts produced saucer-shaped craters with a central peak. Asteroid-sized objects created basins hundreds of kilometers across that have concentric rings of peaks inside. The other planets were similarly bombarded, but their scars are not so obvious. Mercury, like the Moon, has virtually no atmosphere to wear away its craters.

HOW CRATERS ARE FORMED

A meteorite hits at great speed. It blasts a crater in the surface and throws up a blanket of rock.

Some rock falls back, making a rim. A central peak forms if the inside of the crater "bounces back."

The crater becomes saucer-shaped, as the inside fills with debris slipping from the walls.

MOUNTAIN BUILDING

Some of Mercury's mountains and hills owe their existence to impacts. One of the last collisions was probably with an asteroid-sized body, which left a scar 1,300 km across—the Caloris Basin. As well as throwing up concentric rings of mountains around the impact site, the force of the collision sent "Mercury-quake" shocks ripping through and along the surface of the planet. Exactly opposite Caloris there is a range of low hills—the result of shocks buckling the planet's surface.

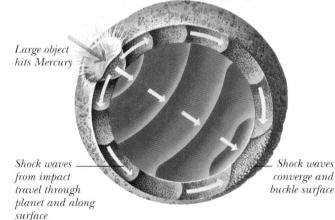

Large object hits Mercury

Shock waves from impact travel through planet and along surface

Shock waves converge and buckle surface

Planet surface labels

Monteverdi, Rubens, Stravinsky, Derzhavin, Vyāsa, Holbein, Velázquez, Al-Hamadhani, Mussorgskij, Kuan-Han-Ch'ing, Praxiteles, Wren, Proust, Li Po, Lermontov, Giotto, Sinan, Vivaldi, Yeats, Handel, Boethius, Polygnotus, Machaut, Thākur, Homer, Titian, Hiroshige, Murasaki, Repin, Renoir, Ibsen, Unkei, Petrarch, Chekov, Nampeyo, Neumann, Ghiberti, Equiano, Bramante, Coleridge, Africanus Horton, Rabelais, Discovery Rupes, Mira Rupes, Boccaccia

MARINER 10

The U.S. probe, launched in November 1973, was the first to visit two planets. After passing Venus it flew on to Mercury, making three close encounters in 1974 and 1975 and mapping most of the planet's surface. It is still in orbit around the Sun.

FACTS AND FIGURES

Diameter	4,878 km
Average distance from Sun	57,910,000 km
Orbital speed around Sun	47.89 km/sec
Circles Sun (a "year")	87.97 days
A "day":	
Turns on axis	58 days 16 hours
Sunrise to sunrise	176 days
Mass (Earth = 1)	0.055
Average density (water = 1)	5.43
Surface gravity (Earth = 1)	0.38
Surface temperature	−180° to +430°C

ACTIVITIES

● It is difficult to spot Mercury because it is a small planet that is always close to the Sun.

● Look in the sunset glow or low in the predawn sky, when the planet's orbit takes it farthest from the Sun.

● With the naked eye, look for a bright, slightly pinkish "star."

● Through binoculars or a telescope, you can see Mercury as a small disk. Like the Moon, it goes through a series of phases.

VENUS

VENUS IS EARTH'S SISTER PLANET: the two worlds are almost identical in size. But Venus is closer to the Sun and is permanently covered with a thick layer of clouds that reflect sunlight away from its surface. Astronomers thought the clouds would protect Venus from the sunlight that makes daytime temperatures on Mercury so high. If so, Venus would be a lush, steamy world—like Earth 300 million years ago. Space probes, however, have unveiled Venus. It is the closest thing to hell in our Solar System: a seething, volcanic world on which a spacefarer would simultaneously suffer acid burns and be suffocated, crushed, and roasted. Venus has suffered a runaway greenhouse effect, making it the hottest of the planets.

A Pioneer-Venus 1 view of the permanently shrouded planet. The clouds are made of droplets of highly corrosive sulfuric acid.

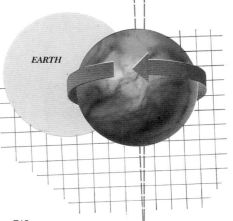

EARTH

WORLD IN REVERSE   2.7°

Compared to the other planets, Venus spins backward. Its axis is tilted 2.7° from the vertical, and the planet takes 243 days to turn once, making its day longer than its year. The atmosphere also rotates, taking 4 days to circle the planet.

STRUCTURE

CRUST

MANTLE

RADIUS: 6,051 KILOMETERS

CORE

INSIDE VENUS

The structure of Venus is similar to Earth: a rocky mantle and crust over a core of iron. But Venus spins slowly, so its iron core does not generate a magnetic field. Its "air" is mostly unbreathable carbon dioxide, with a trace of nitrogen, while sulfur compounds float in the air as clouds and haze. The atmospheric pressure is a crushing 90 times that of Earth.

ATMOSPHERE

OTHER

NITROGEN

CARBON DIOXIDE

VENUS UNVEILED

Several orbiting probes have used radar to map the planet through its clouds. They have discovered that Venus is much flatter than Earth. Volcanic plains extend around the whole planet, but there are some large upland regions. Except for Maxwell Montes and Alpha and Beta Regio, Venus's features have female names.

ISHTAR TERRA

This region of mountains covers an area the size of Australia and its highest point, Maxwell Montes, is a little taller than Earth's Mount Everest. Ishtar also contains the vast, smooth plateau Lakshmi Planum, and the 100-km-wide crater, Cleopatra— almost certainly the result of a meteorite impact.

ISHTAR TERRA

Cleopatra Patera

LAKSHMI PLANUM

Vesta Rupes

Maxwell Montes

Colette

Ut Rupes

Sacajawea

SEDNA PLANITIA

Sif Mons

Gula Mons

Sappho Patera

EIS

A REGIO

GUINEVERE PLANITIA

PLANITIA

PHOEBE REGIO

Hathor Mons

ALPHA REGIO

Eve

LAVINIA PLANITIA

LADA

The greenhouse effect

On Earth, sunlight passes through the atmosphere and warms the surface, which releases this heat in the form of infrared radiation. Most of this heat radiation escapes into space. On the way, however, it has to pass through the lowest level of Earth's atmosphere, the troposphere. Water vapor here absorbs some of the infrared, and this trapped heat helps to keep Earth warm. On Venus, about half of the infrared fails to escape into space. This is because the carbon dioxide in the atmosphere acts like a pane of glass in a greenhouse: it lets light through but doesn't let heat out. Venus, however, would be even hotter than 465°C were it not for the sulfuric acid haze which stops 80% of the sunlight from ever reaching the surface.

Earth

SUNLIGHT

INFRARED

INFRARED

Troposphere

KM
100

90

80

70

60

50

40

30

20

10

Venus

SUNLIGHT

Upper haze (sulfuric acid)

Clouds

Lower haze

Troposphere

INFRARED

INFRARED

PHOEBE REGIO

The mountains of Phoebe Regio mark the edge of Beta Regio (on the other side of the planet). Beta consists of Rhea and Theia Mons, the two biggest volcanoes on Venus. These volcanoes may have been active in recent years.

ALPHA REGIO

A volcanic region about the size of Scandinavia, Alpha contains domes pushed up by thick and sticky lava, as well as cracks caused by hot lava moving around below the surface. The Venus meridian— the zero of longitude—passes through a circular feature, Eve.

Spare-part spacecraft

The U.S. *Magellan* Orbiter craft was put together with spare parts from the *Viking*, *Voyager*, *Galileo*, and *Ulysses* probes—and it has been a great success since its launch in May 1989. It circles Venus every 3 hr 9 min, mapping most of the planet over 243 days (one Venus day). The main instrument is the Synthetic Aperture Radar. The spacecraft's 3.7-meter radar dish emits thousands of radio pulses a second which bounce off the surface. By analyzing the reflections with powerful computers on Earth, scientists can build up a "picture" of the surface, showing detail down to 250 meters across. In addition, *Magellan* carries an altimeter that measures the heights of surface features with an accuracy of 30 meters.

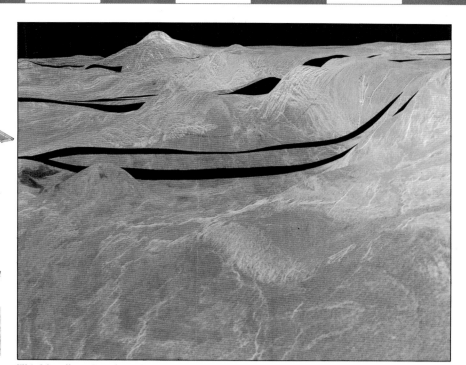

Solar panels *Propulsion module*

Radar dish

Altimeter

Transmitted radar signals

Radio signal from altimeter

Reflected radar signals

Reflected radio signal

SURFACE OF VENUS

This Magellan *view shows how Lakshmi Planum would look from Venus's surface. At right are waterfalls of solidified lava; the 5-km-high mountain Danu Montes is on the horizon. The black stripes are areas that the radar on* Magellan *missed on its "day" of mapping.*

VIOLENT, VOLCANIC VENUS

Scientists hoped that *Magellan* would tell them much about Venus's history—for instance, when the greenhouse effect started. Instead, they discovered that the planet has concealed much of its past with lava flows. Venus is highly volcanic, and is probably still very active. The oval feature (*right*) is Sacajawea Patera, a huge volcanic crater measuring 215 by 120 km. It supplied much of the lava which built up the huge plateau Lakshmi Planum. After filling the plain to overflowing, the supply of molten rock dried up and the floor of the crater sank, cracking the plain. Sacajawea appears as one of two large holes in the smooth expanse of the Lakshmi Planum.

Pavlova

Mead

Hestia Rupes

OVDA REGIO

An area that looks, literally, like nothing on Earth. Its rocks have been cracked, squeezed, and stretched by violent forces. Ovda also contains Venus's largest meteorite crater, the 275-km-wide Mead. Impact craters are a rarity on Venus: eruptions from volcanoes and lava flows have destroyed most of them.

VIEW FROM THE SURFACE

Several Soviet *Venera* craft have survived the very high pressures and temperatures to land on the surface and send back images. In 1982, *Venera 13* (*left*) landed near Beta Regio amid a barren scene of flat volcanic rocks (*below*). The camera scanned the landscape at an angle and parts of the spacecraft, such as a discarded lens cap, appear in the foreground. The dense clouds bathe the scene with an orange light.

APHRODITE TERRA

Roughly the size of the African continent, Aphrodite is the largest upland region on Venus. It is bisected by the huge Diana Chasma, an enormous rift valley 280 km across at its widest— comparable with the Valles Marineris on Mars.

FACTS AND FIGURES

Diameter	**12,103 km**
Average distance from Sun	**108,200,000 km**
Orbital speed around Sun	**35.03 km/sec**
Circles Sun (a "year")	**224.7 days**
A "day":	
Turns on axis	**243.01 days**
Sunrise to sunrise	**117 days**
Mass (Earth = 1)	**0.81**
Average density (water = 1)	**5.25**
Surface gravity (Earth = 1)	**0.9**
Surface temperature	**465°C**

ACTIVITIES

● Venus stays fairly close to the Sun in the sky and is easiest to spot after sunset, as a brilliant "evening star"; or before dawn as a "morning star."

● Like the Moon, Venus shows phases as it circles around the Sun. Try spotting the phases with a small telescope: the easiest one to see is the narrow crescent, when Venus is close to us and nearly in line with the Sun.

● Is Venus so bright that it casts a shadow? If you live in a really dark area, try answering this question.

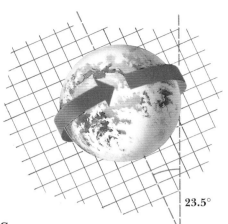

23.5°

EARTH

ALTHOUGH EACH PLANET has its own characteristics, Earth is unique in many ways. Unlike other planets, Earth is "active." By means of volcanoes and earthquakes, our planet "regenerates" its surface so that it is constantly changing. It is the only planet to have liquid water in any quantity: Mars is too cold; Venus, too hot. The atmosphere, too, is quite different from that of any other planet. Unlike the neighboring planets with their carbon-dioxide rich atmospheres, Earth's atmosphere is rich in nitrogen and oxygen. This atmosphere helps to screen out some of the more harmful radiation from the Sun and also shields Earth's surface from impacts by meteorites. The combination of an ever-changing surface, the oceans, and the protective atmosphere has led to the development of something else unique to our planet: life.

SEASONAL TILT
Earth spins once every 24 hours on an axis that is tilted 23.5° from the vertical. This tilt is responsible for Earth's different seasons as it orbits the Sun.

Our planet, photographed by the Apollo 17 astronauts on their way to the Moon. Note the huge icecap over the Antarctic.

S T R U C T U R E A T M O S P H E R E

CRUST
MANTLE
OUTER CORE
INNER CORE

RADIUS: 6,378 KILOMETERS

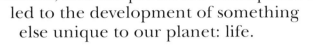

OTHER
WATER VAPOR
OXYGEN
NITROGEN

INSIDE EARTH
In the center is a core of solid iron, with a temperature of 4,000°C, which is surrounded by an outer core of liquid iron that generates Earth's magnetic field. The rocks of the mantle lie above, topped by lighter rocks in the crust. The atmosphere is 77% nitrogen and 21% oxygen, plus a small amount of water vapor and other gases.

WEATHER PATTERNS
A cyclone—a low-pressure weather system—approaches Britain from the Atlantic. The atmosphere and ocean currents both create Earth's weather patterns.

GREENHOUSE EFFECT
Earth's atmosphere acts like a greenhouse to keep the heat in. However, too many "greenhouse gases"—such as carbon dioxide and methane—lead to a buildup of heat, as happened naturally on Venus.

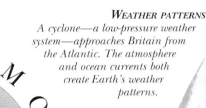

MAGNETOSPHERE
SOLAR WIND
Earth
Van Allen belts
Magnetic field lines
SOLAR WIND

Magnetic bubble
As Earth spins, the iron in its core generates strong electric currents that create a magnetic field. This reaches out into the space surrounding the planet, forming a gigantic magnetic "bubble" called the magnetosphere. The magnetosphere shields Earth from the solar wind—the "gale" of charged particles streaming away from the Sun. These particles become trapped in the magnetic field and concentrated in two huge, doughnut-shaped belts—the Van Allen belts (discovered by the *Explorer 1* and *3* satellites in 1958). The particles can damage the electrical systems on spacecraft as they pass through the belts.

The solar wind blows on the magnetosphere, making it sway in space like a huge jellyfish. But the stream of particles in the solar wind is strong enough to compress the magnetosphere at the front and to draw it out behind into a "magnetotail" rather like a giant wind sock—in this case one that is 500 Earth diameters long.

HOLE AT THE POLE
Earth is wrapped in a layer of ozone gas (a form of oxygen) that protects us from dangerous ultraviolet radiation from the Sun. Unfortunately, as a result of pollution by humans, the ozone layer has thinned out over Antarctica, and there are signs that it is thinning out over the North Pole.

Continents in collision

Earth's crust is made of separate pieces, or plates, which are driven around the globe by heat currents within the planet's interior. Since the continents ride on the top of these plates, the distribution of land is constantly changing. About 200 million years ago, all the land was grouped in one supercontinent, Pangea, which then separated to form the modern continents. Molten rock emerging from ridges that run through all the oceans continues to drive plates apart, at a rate similar to that at which a fingernail grows. Where plates collide—such as around the edge of the Pacific—the surface buckles, mountain ranges are pushed up, and earthquakes and volcanoes occur as rock is forced back into the mantle. Through this process, known as "plate tectonics," Earth constantly renews itself.

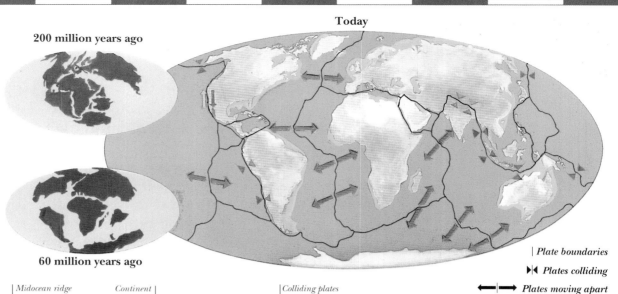

200 million years ago

Today

60 million years ago

| Plate boundaries

▶◀ Plates colliding

◀— —▶ Plates moving apart

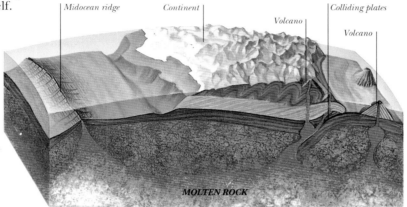

Midocean ridge   *Continent*   *Colliding plates*

Volcano

Volcano

MOLTEN ROCK

PLATE TECTONICS AT WORK

In this cross section of Earth's crust, molten rock is seeping up along a midocean ridge (*shown on the left*), which marks the boundary of two plates. The rock solidifies to create new crust on the ocean floor, pushing the adjacent plates apart. On the right, a plate is in collision with another, throwing up mountain ranges as the surface buckles. Colliding plates are also the site of earthquakes and volcanoes as crust is pushed into the mantle and destroyed. Note the undersea volcanoes, which develop into islands.

THE BLUE PLANET

Seen from space, Earth easily earns its nickname of "The Blue Planet." Two-thirds is covered by liquid water.

PROTECTIVE LAYER

The atmosphere is thin— 75% of it lies within 15 km of the surface—but it protects life from most of the harmful radiation from space, as well as from meteoroids.

SUNNY SAHARA

The Sahara receives overhead sunshine for much of the year because of Earth's tilt. That is why it is so hot and dry.

WATERWORKS

Much of the surface of Earth is sculpted by wind and, especially, by water. Waves battering the coast create steep cliffs and pinnacles; rivers erode rock to make spectacular canyons, such as the Grand Canyon (*right*); and icy glaciers carve away mountains. Water can also create land, as when slow-moving rivers such as the Mississippi (*below*) deposit sediments when they reach the sea.

Grand Canyon: A stream cutting through the soft, layered sandstone and limestone of Arizona created the enormous Grand Canyon. It is now 1.9 km at its deepest.

Mississippi Delta: Heavy with silty sediments picked up on its journey across the U.S., the Mississippi River empties into the Gulf of Mexico. The slow-moving river has built up a delta of sediment where it enters the sea, creating new land where none existed before.

EARTH PROBE

In the early 1990s, the Galileo *space probe made two very close flybys of Earth—coming within 960 km of the surface—on its way to Jupiter. This was in order to pick up speed to reach the giant planet; but* Galileo *also photographed Earth and its Moon in close-up.*

FACTS AND FIGURES

Diameter	12,756 km
Average distance from Sun	149,600,000 km
Orbital speed around Sun	29.79 km/sec
Circles Sun (a "year")	365.26 days
A day:	
Turns on axis	23 hours 56 minutes
Sunrise to sunrise	24 hours
Mass (Earth = 1)	1
Average density (water = 1)	5.52
Surface gravity (Earth = 1)	1
Surface temperature	−70°C to +55°C

ACTIVITIES

● Observe Earth's spin: follow the shadow of a pointer across a sundial as Earth rotates (*also see page 43*).

● Capture Earth's spin on film: a long-exposure (about 15 min) photograph on a clear night will show "star trails" caused by Earth's rotation.

● As Earth orbits the Sun, it faces different directions in space, revealing different stars with each season. Use the star maps on pages 46–49 to chart Earth's yearly course around the Sun.

MARS

OF ALL THE PLANETS, Mars is the one that most resembles Earth. A "Mars day" is almost the same length as ours, and Mars has mountains, deserts, white polar caps, volcanoes, and gaping canyons. It is the only planet that scientists have seriously considered as a possible site for extra-terrestrial life. Last century, some astronomers reported "canals" crisscrossing the planet's surface and suggested Martians had built them to irrigate their parched world. Changing dark patches on the surface were thought to be vegetation. We now know that the "canals" are optical illusions and that the patches appear when dark rocks lose their covering of sand in stormy weather.

Gashed world: the Valles Marineris canyon dominates this view of Mars. The three "pimples" are huge volcanoes.

Earth

25.2°

EARTH'S LITTLE BROTHER

Mars is just over half the size of Earth, its day is 41 minutes longer, and its axis is tilted by just 1.7° more. The seasons on Mars and Earth are also similar, although each Martian season is twice as long.

S T R U C T U R E

RADIUS: 3,393 KILOMETERS

CRUST
MANTLE
CORE

A T M O S P H E R E

OTHER
ARGON
NITROGEN

CARBON
DIOXIDE

INSIDE MARS

The iron core is small and probably solid—if the core were liquid it would generate a magnetic field and there is no detectable magnetism on Mars. Covering the core is a rocky mantle, topped by a solid crust. The thin atmosphere (less than 1% of Earth's) is made almost entirely of carbon dioxide.

THARSIS BULGE
Lava accumulating below volcanoes in the Tharsis region—including the giant Olympus, Ascraeus, Pavonis, and Arsia volcanoes—has caused an 8,000 km wide swelling. Just to the north is Alba Patera, Mars's most extensive volcano. It is 1,600 km wide but only 6 km high.

BARREN DESERT
The red plains, or planitia, are literally rusty. Close-up pictures reveal dried-up riverbeds where water once flowed. This water reacted with iron in the soil to make rust.

Mighty Olympus Mons

The biggest volcano in the Solar System is Olympus Mons. Like many of the volcanoes on Mars, it is shaped like a huge shield, with gently sloping sides. On Earth, shield volcanoes form when successive plumes of molten rock gush up from the interior. The Martian volcanoes, however, are much bigger: compare Olympus Mons with the Hawaiian Islands and Mauna Loa, the largest volcano on Earth. The constantly moving crust on Earth carries volcanoes away from their source of molten rock. Olympus Mons stayed fixed above the active volcanic area and continued to grow for millions of years. All Mars's volcanoes are thought to be extinct now.

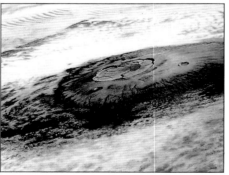

At 26 km, Olympus Mons is three times higher than Mount Everest. The base of the "shield" is wide enough to cover Arizona, while the crater on top could swallow New York City twice over.

VALLES MARINERIS
This canyon system stretches for more than 4,000 km—10 times longer than the Grand Canyon. In places the canyons are 200 km wide and 7 km deep.

Map labels:
VASTITAS BOREALIS
ARCADIA PLANITIA
AMAZONIS PLANITIA
Tharsis Montes
Valles Marineris
SYRIA PLANUM
SINAI PLANUM
SOLIS PLANUM
Alba Fossae
Tantalus Fossae
Mareotis Fossae
Tempe Fossae
Milankovic
Alba Patera
Uranius Tholus
Ceraunius Tholus
Tharsis Tholus
Olympus Mons
Ascraeus Mons
Pavonis Mons
Arsia Mons
Tithonium Chasma
Ius Chasma
Sirenum Fossae
Phaenna Fossae

SOUTHERN WINTER
The south polar cap is at its maximum, covered with water and carbon dioxide ices. In summer, there will be only a thin coating of water ice.

Summit: 26.4 km above the Martian lowlands

Mauna Loa: 9.1 km above the ocean floor

Olympus Mons

Sea level

Ocean floor

Hawaiian Islands

Potato moons

Mars is orbited by two potato-shaped moons: Phobos and Deimos. Because they are so small—Phobos is 28 km in length and Deimos just 16 km—they were not discovered until 1877. Both are almost certainly asteroids that Mars managed to capture from the nearby belt of "minor planets." Like most moons, they do not have an atmosphere, but both have sufficient gravitational pull to hang on to a thin powdering of dust that probably comes from meteorite impacts.

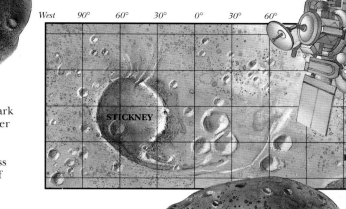

WEATHER ON MARS
A swirl of clouds high in the thin atmosphere indicates the beginnings of a storm system. Like Earth, Mars has several different types of clouds in its atmosphere.

DEIMOS
Made of extremely dark rock, Deimos has fewer large craters than Phobos. Its surface is also smoother and less fractured than that of its companion.

AROUND THE RED PLANET
Although Phobos and Deimos both circle Mars, they do so in different orbits. The radius of Deimos's orbit is 23,460 km from the center of Mars—about seven times the radius of Mars itself (*see scale below*). Phobos orbits a mere 9,380 km from Mars—or just short of three times the planet's radius. Deimos takes about 30 hours to orbit Mars, compared with the 7 hours 40 minutes that Phobos takes. Because Phobos orbits Mars in less than the planet's "day," it appears to go backward across the sky. Phobos is being pulled inward by Mars's gravity and should collide with the planet in about 50 million years' time.

PHOBOS
The *Viking 1* Orbiter flew within 500 km of Phobos, revealing a rocky, heavily cratered surface (*above*). Stickney, the largest crater, is nearly 10 km across. In 1989, the Soviet *Phobos* probe (*inset*) was to have returned detailed images taken 50 meters from the surface. Unfortunately, the Soviets lost contact with their craft after it had sent back just 40 images taken between 200 and 400 km from the moon.

VIKING ORBITERS
The two Orbiters circled Mars for several years, making a thorough survey of its surface and relaying the discoveries from the Landers back to Earth.

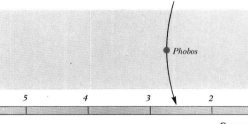

Deimos   Phobos

8   7   6   5   4   3   2   1

SCALE IN RADII OF MARS

CRATERED TERRAIN
Mars was heavily bombarded with objects from space. Wind has eroded many craters, but some have remained almost unchanged for millions of years. This is because Mars, unlike Earth, does not have plate tectonics changing its surface.

VIKING LANDERS
The Viking Lander (left) is the most sophisticated space probe to visit another world. Two Landers were sent to different locations in the northern hemisphere; both had sensors to "touch," "smell," "see," and "taste" the Martian soil, test it for signs of life, and monitor the planet's weather. Parts of Viking 2, which took the picture above, can be seen in the foreground. The metal object (right) is a soil scoop, which dug the nearby trenches in its search for life.

VIKING MISSIONS
Two *Viking* craft were sent to Mars to search for life. On arrival in 1976, the Orbiters began to circle Mars, while the Landers touched down on the planet's surface. Their first experiments with soil samples produced gases, which suggested that living cells were present. Later, scientists realized that the gases came from highly reactive chemicals in the soil. In fact, such chemicals would serve to kill off any life!

DUST STORM
A dust storm begins to gather over the Argyre Planitia. Sometimes, as in 1971, dust storms cover the entire planet. They tend to take place shortly after Mars, which has an elliptical orbit, has made its closest approach to the Sun.

FACTS AND FIGURES

Diameter	**6,786 km**
Average distance from Sun	**227,940,000 km**
Orbital speed around Sun	**24.13 km/sec**
Circles Sun (a "year")	**686.98 days**
A day:	
Turns on axis	**24 hours 37 minutes**
Sunrise to sunrise	**24 hours 38 minutes**
Mass (Earth = 1)	**0.11**
Average density (water = 1)	**3.95**
Surface gravity (Earth = 1)	**0.38**
Surface temperature	**−120°C to +25°C**

ACTIVITIES

● Mars is easy to spot in the night sky, because it is usually bright and red. See if you can follow its path against the stars for several months—sometimes it seems to loop back for a few weeks as Earth overtakes it.

● With a small telescope, you should just be able to see one of the polar caps and some of the dark patches.

● A medium or large telescope will let you see more surface markings. Hazy patches may indicate where a giant dust storm is brewing.

JUPITER

After the sun, Jupiter is king of the Solar System. It is bigger than all the other planets put together, and could easily contain 1,300 bodies the size of Earth. Compared with the small, rocky inner planets, Jupiter is like a giant gasbag made up almost entirely of hydrogen and helium. At the top of the atmosphere, the gas forms striped layers of red-brown and yellow-ochre clouds. Below, the gas becomes more compressed until it turns into liquid. Eventually, it becomes so compressed that it looks and behaves like a metal. Jupiter's core is very hot—35,000°C—and the planet gives off twice as much heat as it receives from the Sun. Had Jupiter been 50 times more massive, its core would have been hot enough to fuse hydrogen, and Jupiter would have become a star.

The biggest planet: gas giant Jupiter is all atmosphere and no surface. Its colorful clouds are bands of violent storms.

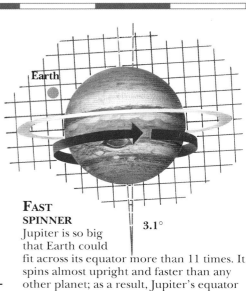

FAST SPINNER
Jupiter is so big that Earth could fit across its equator more than 11 times. It spins almost upright and faster than any other planet; as a result, Jupiter's equator bulges outward, giving it an oval shape.

3.1°

Earth

NORTH POLAR REGION
This is the least detailed area on Jupiter. The rest of the planet consists of belts (dark regions) and zones (light regions) of banded gas.

NORTH TEMPERATE BELT
This is the most northerly of the major belts. Its southern edge is sometimes bordered by "red ovals"—eddies in the atmosphere almost half the size of Earth.

STRUCTURE

RADIUS: 71,492 KILOMETERS

ATMOSPHERE

LIQUID HYDROGEN

METALLIC HYDROGEN

CORE

INSIDE JUPITER
Most of the planet consists of hydrogen in gaseous, liquid, and metallic form, although there is a small, rocky core. The atmosphere is also mainly hydrogen, with some helium, plus traces of methane and ammonia.

OTHER

HELIUM

HYDROGEN

ATMOSPHERE

A FINE RING
Discovered in January 1979 by Voyager 1, Jupiter's ring is extremely thin and faint. An even dimmer "halo" extends in toward the cloud tops. Both consist of dark grains of dust no bigger than particles of smoke.

Great Red Spot
Lying in the South Tropical Zone, the Great Red Spot is a giant storm some 40,000 km across—three times the size of Earth. Within this area of high pressure, upward-spiraling winds carry gases to great heights in the atmosphere, where they react with sunlight. The red color is due to phosphorus released as part of this reaction. Although the spot sometimes fades, it has been a feature of Jupiter for at least 300 years.

Io

ACTIVITIES

● Jupiter is easy to spot because it shines brighter than any star. Only the Moon and Venus are brighter.

● Use binoculars to see up to four tiny points of light—the Galilean moons—along the line of Jupiter's equator. Their positions change from night to night as they orbit the planet.

● A small telescope reveals how Jupiter is flattened at the poles. Observe the dark cloud belts across the yellowish disk, which can change daily.

TWIN VOYAGERS
Two space probes arrived in 1979, having survived their close encounters with Jupiter's radiation belts. Voyager 1 flew by 277,500 km above the cloud tops in March; Voyager 2 followed in July at a height of 650,000 km.

A family of moons

Like all the giant planets, Jupiter is surrounded by a family of moons. Of the 16 moons known, four—Io, Europa, Ganymede, and Callisto—are giants among moons. All are larger than the planet Pluto, and Ganymede outstrips Mercury. They are called the Galilean moons after the Italian astronomer Galileo Galilei, who discovered them in 1610. The other 12 moons are all small—ranging from Amalthea, at 270 km across, to Leda with a diameter of just 16 km.

GANYMEDE

At 5,260 km across, Ganymede is the largest moon in the Solar System. The icy crust is heavily cratered, scarred from being bombarded in the early days of the Solar System. But the surface is also crisscrossed with complex ridges and grooves—signs of more recent torture.

Plumes of sulfur compounds rise from Io's volcanoes.

EUROPA

Smoother than a billiard ball, the smallest of Jupiter's four large moons (diameter 3,140 km) is the least understood. Scientists think that Europa is wrapped in a deep layer of ice—underneath which may lie a huge ocean.

IO

Looking like a cosmic pizza, the red, orange, and yellow splotches on Io (diameter 3,630 km) come from plumes shooting 300 km upward from volcanoes. Io is one of only two moons with active volcanoes. There are also powerful electric currents flowing between Io and Jupiter—caused by the planet's magnetic field.

Valhalla

CALLISTO

Densely packed with impact craters, there are no "plains" on the surface of this moon (diameter 4,800 km). Valhalla, 300 km across, is the biggest of all the craters. Callisto resembles our Moon, but with craters made of ice instead of rocks.

NORTH TROPICAL ZONE
The brightest of the zones. These bands are made of clouds lying at higher levels than those making up the belts. Their white color comes from ammonia crystals.

NORTH EQUATORIAL BELT
The twisted structure is caused by violent winds. Jupiter's winds are complex, with adjacent belts and zones having winds blowing in opposite directions.

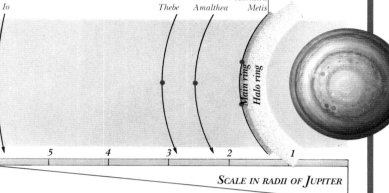

SCALE IN RADII OF JUPITER

Farthest moon: 23.7 million km from Jupiter

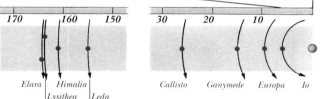

340	320	310	300	290

Sinope   *Pasiphae*   *Carme*   *Ananke*

170	160	150

Elara   *Himalia*   *Leda*
Lysithea

30	20	10

Callisto   *Ganymede*   *Europa*   *Io*

AROUND JUPITER

The 16 moons fall into three groups (*see above*). Close to the planet, but outside the rings, are Metis, Adrastea, Amalthea, and Thebe. They orbit at between 128,000 and 220,000 km from the center of the planet (between 1.8 and 3.1 on the scale above). Apart from Amalthea, the inner moons are newly discovered satellites about which we know little. Then, from 420,000 to 1.9 million km, come the Galilean giants of Io, Europa, Ganymede, and Callisto. The other eight moons are tiny—only Himalia measures more than 100 km across. Four orbit the planet at between 11 and 12 million km; they are probably fragments of ice and rock left over from Jupiter's birth. The outermost four moons go around the planet in a direction opposite to the others at between 21 and 24 million km. Almost certainly they are bodies captured from the asteroid belt by Jupiter's gravity.

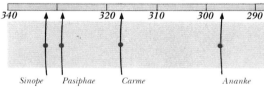

Europa

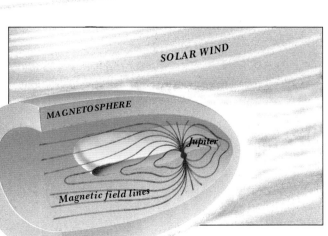

Mighty magnet

Jupiter's fast-spinning layer of metallic hydrogen acts like a dynamo to generate a powerful magnetic field. The field lines form a gigantic "bubble" around the planet—the magnetosphere—which is 1,200 times bigger than the one surrounding Earth. The magnetosphere traps fast-moving electrically charged particles from the solar wind, forming belts of radiation that are a hazard to spacecraft. The solar wind blows the magnetosphere back into a long "tail" that stretches beyond Saturn.

SOUTH POLAR REGION
This complex area of turbulent clouds is often home to "white ovals"—enormous, temporary storm systems.

FACTS AND FIGURES	
Diameter (equatorial)	142,984 km
Diameter (polar)	133,708 km
Average distance from the Sun	778,330,000 km
Orbital speed around the Sun	13.06 km/sec
Circles Sun (a "year")	11.86 years
A "day": Turns on axis / Sunrise to sunrise	9 hours 55 minutes
Mass (Earth = 1)	318
Average density (water = 1)	1.33
Surface gravity (Earth = 1)	2.64
Temperature at cloud tops	−150°C

SATURN

ALTHOUGH ALL THE GAS GIANTS are encircled by rings, Saturn will always be known as *the* planet with rings. But while the rings of the other planets are dark, Saturn's are dazzlingly bright and wide. Three are easily visible through a telescope and stretch across a distance almost as great as that between Earth and our Moon. Saturn holds the record for the largest number of moons in the Solar System: 18 at the last count, with a further six suspected. But the planet itself is relatively unexciting. Apart from outbreaks of white spots in 1933, 1960, and 1990 (caused by huge, violent storms), the disk is usually featureless and hazy. Saturn has the distinction of having the lowest density of all the planets: if placed on a huge sea, it would float.

Showpiece of the Solar System, photographed from a distance of 3.4 million km by the departing Voyager 2 spacecraft.

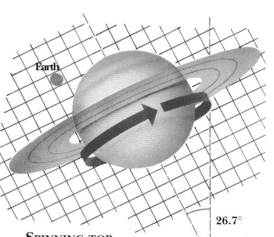

SPINNING TOP
Saturn follows Jupiter's example and has a rapid rate of spin. Its "day" lasts only 10 hours 40 minutes. And, also like Jupiter, it bulges outward at the equator. The planet's axis is tilted 26.7° from the vertical, slightly more than Earth's.

STRUCTURE ATMOSPHERE

ATMOSPHERE

LIQUID HYDROGEN

METALLIC HYDROGEN

CORE

RADIUS: 60,268 KILOMETERS

INSIDE SATURN
Almost completely made of hydrogen and helium, Saturn is very like Jupiter in structure. Its rocky core is probably larger, but because it is less compressed than Jupiter, it has less metallic hydrogen (and therefore a smaller magnetic field).

OTHER

HELIUM

HYDROGEN

WINDY PLANET
This wavy cloud feature marks the boundary between two wind currents flowing in opposite directions. Saturn is one of the windiest planets, with winds reaching 1,800 km/hr at the equator.

Ringworld
Space probes have revealed the extent of Saturn's rings. The A, B, and C rings are visible from Earth; although only tens of meters thick, their span is 274,000 km. These rings are divided into literally thousands of fine ringlets, like the grooves on a record. We now know of a further four rings, including the difficult-to-observe G ring and an extremely faint E ring—300,000 km wide and spanning a distance of 960,000 km.

THE A RING
The outermost of the rings visible from Earth contains the Encke Division, a narrow gap where the innermost moon orbits.

THE B RING
The broadest, brightest, and densest ring is crossed by dark, radial "spokes"—probably clouds of fine dust above the rings, channeled into lines by electric fields.

THE F RING
Outermost of the bright rings, the narrow F ring was discovered by Pioneer 11 in 1979.

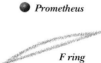

Prometheus

F ring

Pandora

PLAITED RINGS
Parts of the F ring consist of two ringlets twisted around one another. This is thought to be caused by the gravity of Pandora and Prometheus, two tiny "shepherd" moons that "nose" the ring particles into line like a flock of sheep.

ANNE'S SPOT
A large oval feature, discovered by Voyager scientist Anne Bunker. It is similar to, although much smaller than, Jupiter's Great Red Spot.

Saturnian satellites

Saturn has the largest family of moons in the Solar System—18 discovered so far. With the exception of Titan, the moons are made of ice. Many have been heavily bombarded with meteorites, some so large that the impact must nearly have broken the moons up. In fact, Janus and Epimetheus—known as the co-orbitals because they share an orbit—are two parts of a larger body. The gravitational pull of Saturn's moons has a great effect on the shape of the planet's rings.

TITAN

Second largest moon in the Solar System (diameter 5,150 km), Titan is the only moon known to have a dense atmosphere. The thick orange atmosphere consists mainly of nitrogen, suggesting that Titan might be "an Earth in deep freeze." There may be oceans of liquid "natural gas" below the clouds.

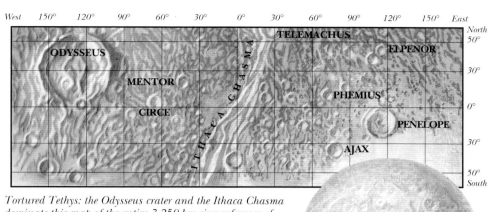

Tortured Tethys: the Odysseus crater and the Ithaca Chasma dominate this map of the entire 3,250 km circumference of Tethys. The chasm, a giant trench stretching 2,000 km, may be the result of an impact or, perhaps, past earthquakes.

MIMAS

Tiny Mimas is dominated by the crater Herschel which measures 135 km across—the moon itself is only 390 km across. It is hard to understand how Mimas could have survived such a great collision.

Herschel

Odysseus

THE CASSINI DIVISION

Discovered in 1675, this appears to be a gap separating the A and B rings. The Voyagers, however, found at least a hundred faint ringlets within the division.

THE C RING

Nicknamed the "Crepe ring," the faintest of the rings visible from Earth is also the bluest. It contains many narrow ringlets.

THE D RING

So close that it almost touches the planet, the D ring is very faint.

TETHYS

Looking like a bigger version of Mimas, icy Tethys is also dominated by a giant impact crater. Odysseus is 400 km in diameter, Tethys 1,050 km. The impact may have broken up Tethys temporarily—as may have happened to Mimas—causing fragments of debris to feed into Saturn's ring system. The Ithaca Chasma, which runs from north to south, is 2,000 km long, 100 km wide, and 5 km deep—far bigger than the Grand Canyon system on Earth.

AROUND SATURN

Saturn's 18 confirmed satellites circle the planet in groups (*see right*). Closest in are the smaller Atlas (which shepherds the A ring), and Prometheus and Pandora (the F-ring shepherds). Also in this group is an unnamed, newly discovered moon. Several of the larger moons in the outer groups also share orbits—probably because they once made up a single body. Phoebe, the outermost moon, orbits Saturn in a direction opposite to the others.

Dione / Helene   *Tethys / Telesto / Calypso*   *Enceladus*   *Mimas*   *Epimetheus / Janus / Prometheus / Pandora / Atlas / New moon*

E ring   G ring   F ring   A ring   B ring   C ring   D ring

7   6   5   4   3   2   1

SCALE IN RADII OF SATURN

Farthest moon: 12.95 million km from Saturn

220   210   200   70   60   50   40   30   20   10

Phoebe   *Iapetus*   *Hyperion*   *Titan*   *Rhea*   *Dione / Helene*

VOYAGING TO SATURN

The Voyager flybys of 1980 and 1981 changed our views of the ringworld.

THE RINGS IN CLOSE-UP

Although the rings look solid, they are made of billions of chunks of ice, ranging in size from ice cubes to blocks the size of a car. They may be material left over from Saturn's birth or pieces of a moon that came too close to the planet.

FACTS AND FIGURES

Diameter (equatorial)	120,536 km
Diameter (polar)	108,728 km
Average distance from Sun	1,426,980,000 km
Orbital speed around Sun	9.64 km/sec
Circles Sun (a "year")	29.46 years
A "day": Turns on axis / Sunrise to sunrise	10 hours 40 minutes
Mass (Earth = 1)	95.18
Average density (water = 1)	0.69
Surface gravity (Earth = 1)	0.925
Temperature at cloud tops	–180°C

ACTIVITIES

● Check on a star chart for Saturn's position; it is easily mistaken for a star.

● Powerful binoculars will reveal the planet's rings, but just barely.

● Use a small telescope to see the rings, encircling what appears to be an illuminated disk hanging in the blackness of space. Look, too, for Titan, the largest of its moons.

● In 1995 and early 1996, Saturn will appear ringless—the rings will be "edge on" to Earth.

URANUS

THE FIRST PLANET to be discovered since ancient times was Uranus. In 1781 William Herschel, an amateur astronomer based in England, was carrying out a survey of the sky when he spotted a greenish disk. At first he thought it was a comet, but its movement showed it to be a planet twice as far away as Saturn. Astronomers were able to work out that Uranus is another gas giant, smaller than Jupiter and Saturn but still four times larger than Earth. Herschel himself discovered two moons circling the planet, and later astronomers found three more. One of the most remarkable things about Uranus is that it is tipped over, effectively circling the Sun on its side. In 1977, scientists found a set of dark, narrow rings around the planet. And that was about the extent of our knowledge of Uranus until *Voyager 2* reached the planet in 1986.

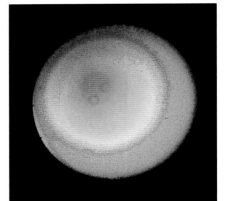

Bull's-eye: shot by Voyager 2 from a distance of 9 million km. The colors have been exaggerated to bring out details.

TIPPED-OVER PLANET
Uranus spins every 17 hours 14 minutes on an axis angled at 97.9° from the vertical—a planet on its side. It is four times bigger than Earth.

Earth

97.9°

ALL IN A HAZE
The upper atmosphere, exposed to the Sun, appears to be covered by a thin haze of "natural gas"—acetylene and methane.

STRUCTURE

RADIUS: 25,559 KILOMETERS

ATMOSPHERE

WATER, AMMONIA, AND METHANE

CORE

INSIDE URANUS
A gaseous mix of ammonia, water, and methane is wrapped around a rocky core. Unlike the other gas giants, though, Uranus generates little or no internal heat (which probably means the planet is not contracting). The atmosphere is mainly hydrogen, with some helium and methane.

ATMOSPHERE

METHANE

HELIUM

HYDROGEN

VOYAGE INTO THE UNKNOWN
Voyager 2 is the only spacecraft to have visited Uranus. It arrived on January 24, 1986, after a journey lasting nearly 8½ years, and flew past at just 81,600 km above the cloud tops.

A BLAND PLANET
Uranus is the most featureless planet we know. Voyager 2 spotted a few small clouds, which showed that the planet has winds of up to 300 km/hr.

Long-lasting seasons
As the planet follows its 84-year orbit around the Sun, the poles point toward and away from the Sun, giving rise to the seasons. But because of the extreme tilt of Uranus, its seasons are exaggerated. Each pole in turn receives 42 years of continuous sunlight, followed by 42 years of darkness. Currently, the southern hemisphere is midway through its summer. So little sunlight reaches Uranus, however, that summer and winter temperatures are within 2°C of each other.

1966
North

1985
North

2030
North

2007
North

MAGNETIC MUDDLE
Voyager 2 discovered a magnetic field similar in strength to that of Earth. However, the magnetic axis is tilted at an angle of 60° to the axis of rotation—as if Earth's north magnetic pole were in Morocco. What's more, the magnetism is generated some 10,000 km from the planet's core—probably by electric currents in the thick mantle of water and ammonia.

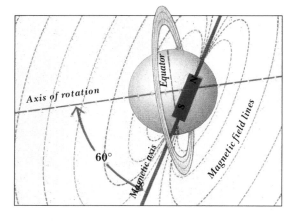

Axis of rotation

Equator

60°

Magnetic axis

Magnetic field lines

Dark rings
Rings were discovered in 1977 when Uranus passed in front of a star. Nine rings were revealed as each in turn blocked the star's light. *Voyager 2* located two more rings. Most of the rings are incredibly narrow (less than 10 km wide) and seem to be made of meter-sized boulders. They are also very dark—some of the blackest material in the Solar System.

A Voyager 2 image of the rings.

Uranian moons

Before *Voyager*, scientists knew of Oberon, Titania, Umbriel, Ariel, and Miranda. Apart from Miranda, which is only 470 km across, they are of significant size, ranging from Ariel (1,160 km) to Titania (1,580 km). *Voyager* went on to discover a further ten moons, all less than 150 km across. Like Saturn, Uranus has "shepherd" moons: Cordelia and Ophelia keep the particles of the slightly oval-shaped outer ring in place. Although it was exciting to discover new moons, it was not unexpected. But scientists had not suspected the amazing features *Voyager* would reveal on the five original moons. In contrast to Uranus, the parent planet, their surfaces were amazingly rich in detail.

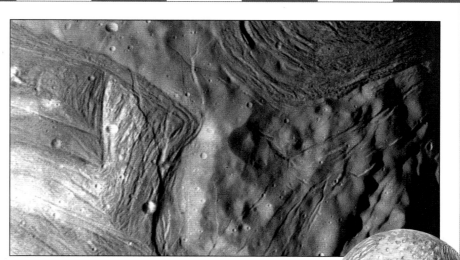

A moon built by committee? Examples of features from nearly every other body in the Solar System are found on Miranda.

ARIEL

An icy surface is crisscrossed by a network of grooves up to 30 km deep, but there are relatively few craters. It seems that many of the craters have been "resurfaced" by recent volcanic activity.

MIRANDA

This moon is a jumble of grooves, craters, cliffs, and smoother areas apparently flung together haphazardly. Although less than 500 km across, Miranda has canyons ten times deeper than Earth's Grand Canyon. Scientists believe Miranda was blasted apart by an enormous impact but later reassembled itself.

UMBRIEL

The darkest of the major moons (it is 10 km bigger than Ariel), Umbriel is one of the most heavily cratered. Unlike its neighbors, Umbriel's surface shows no sign of recent activity. One very unusual feature is the bright-rimmed crater, Wunda, which is 110 km across.

AROUND URANUS

While the major moons circle the planet between 130,000 and 583,000 km out (*see right*), the newly discovered moons are much closer in. All the moons orbit in the same direction as the planet rotates.

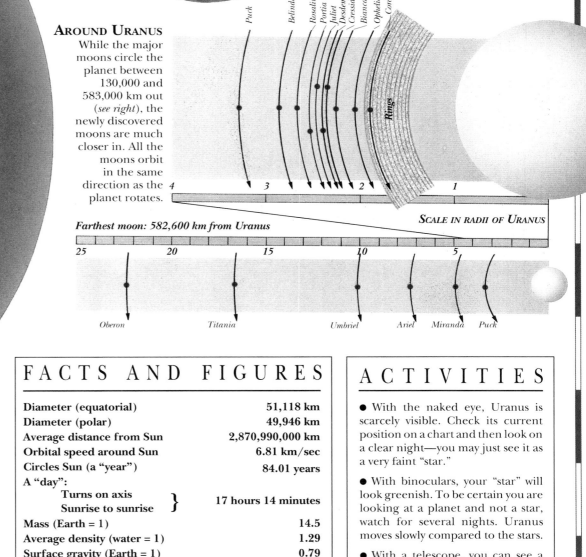

Farthest moon: 582,600 km from Uranus

SCALE IN RADII OF URANUS

Puck Belinda Rosalind Portia Juliet Desdemona Cressida Bianca Ophelia Cordelia Ring

Oberon   Titania   Umbriel   Ariel   Miranda   Puck

FACTS AND FIGURES

Diameter (equatorial)	51,118 km
Diameter (polar)	49,946 km
Average distance from Sun	2,870,990,000 km
Orbital speed around Sun	6.81 km/sec
Circles Sun (a "year")	84.01 years
A "day": Turns on axis / Sunrise to sunrise	17 hours 14 minutes
Mass (Earth = 1)	14.5
Average density (water = 1)	1.29
Surface gravity (Earth = 1)	0.79
Temperature at cloud tops	–210°C

ACTIVITIES

● With the naked eye, Uranus is scarcely visible. Check its current position on a chart and then look on a clear night—you may just see it as a very faint "star."

● With binoculars, your "star" will look greenish. To be certain you are looking at a planet and not a star, watch for several nights. Uranus moves slowly compared to the stars.

● With a telescope, you can see a disk, but no features.

NEPTUNE

NEPTUNE OWES ITS DISCOVERY to the power of mathematics. After Uranus was discovered, astronomers realized that the planet was being pulled slightly off course by an unknown gravitational force—perhaps another planet lying farther out. Two mathematicians, John Couch Adams in England and Urbain Leverrier in France, independently calculated where the missing planet should be. It was found, right on target, by Johann Galle in Berlin in 1846. Astronomers later discovered two moons circling Neptune. One was distinctly odd: a large moon orbiting in a direction opposite to the planet's rotation. Otherwise, Neptune remained mysterious. It was too far away to show markings, and astronomers were not sure if there were rings until *Voyager 2* arrived there in 1989.

Hazy planet: a false-color image shows a haze (red) overlying the methane atmosphere.

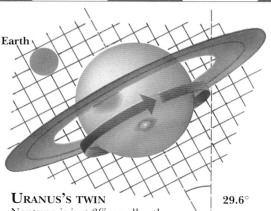

Earth

URANUS'S TWIN   29.6°
Neptune is just 3% smaller than Uranus, and its day is 67 minutes shorter. But it is almost upright in comparison—the axis is only slightly more tilted from the vertical than ours.

THE BLUE PLANET
Apart from Earth, Neptune is the bluest planet in the Solar System. Its atmosphere is flecked with white clouds of methane ice.

STRUCTURE ATMOSPHERE

RADIUS: 24,764 KILOMETERS

ATMOSPHERE

WATER, AMMONIA, AND METHANE

CORE

INSIDE NEPTUNE
Like Uranus, Neptune has a small rocky core. This is covered by an enormous ocean of warm water and gases. The atmosphere is mostly hydrogen, with a little helium and methane.

HYDROGEN

METHANE

HELIUM

A fourth ringworld

Although astronomers suspected that Neptune had partial rings, or "arcs," *Voyager 2* revealed the complete ring system. It found four rings—two broad and two narrow—surrounding the planet. The rings are made of extremely small particles, which in some places clump together. It was three clumps in the outermost ring that gave the appearance of arcs as seen from Earth. How these clumps persist is not known: the particles should spread out evenly around the ring.

INNER SHEPHERDS
Two newly discovered moons shepherd particles at the inner edge of the two narrow rings. Galatea, only 150 km across, looks after the outer ring. Despoina, 180 km across, acts as shepherd for the second thin ring.

HURRICANE WINDS
Winds race around the planet in a direction opposite to its rotation, sweeping the two dark spots backward. The Scooter is deeper in the atmosphere and less affected by winds: relative to the dark spots, it seems to "scoot" forward.

GREAT DARK SPOT
A huge storm system, the size of Earth, dominates Neptune. Winds blow around the spot in a westerly direction at speeds of 2,000 km an hour—the fastest in the Solar System.

THE SCOOTER
This cirrus-cloud feature scoots around Neptune in just 16.8 hrs. It changed shape from round to square to triangular during the Voyager encounter.

Neptunian moons

Before the arrival of *Voyager 2*, we knew of two moons in orbit around Neptune: the 2,700-km diameter Triton and the much smaller Nereid, just 340 km across. *Voyager* discovered a further six. One of these, Larissa, was seen from Earth in 1981 but was thought to be a portion of Neptune's rings. Most of the new moons are less than 200 km across and may be fragments of larger moons that broke up. *Voyager* flew too far from Nereid to image it in any detail but approached to within 40,000 km of Triton, sending back breathtaking pictures.

PROTEUS

At 400 km across, the largest of the newly discovered moons. It is heavily cratered—one crater is nearly half as big as Proteus itself.

TRITON

The coldest object in the Solar System (an icy −235°C), Triton's appearance has been altered by violent volcanic activity. Its surface has melted and refrozen repeatedly, causing a network of huge cracks.

Summertime at Triton's south pole. The pink is probably due to methane ice, which, bombarded by cosmic rays, has formed complex organic chemicals.

BROAD RINGS
An inner broad ring stretches for 11,000 km. A second ring—5,500 km wide—lies between the two narrow rings.

NARROW RINGS
The two narrow, brighter rings are made of very dark particles which form clumps in the outer ring. Both rings have inner shepherds but seem to lack outer ones.

VOLCANOES OF ICE

The black streaks at Triton's south pole are volcanoes—some still active. Like geysers on Earth, Triton's volcanoes spew out vapor (nitrogen) mixed with black dust. Here, a plume rises 8 km, where winds carry it for 150 km. The plumes coat Triton's surface with dark streaks and contribute to its very thin atmosphere of nitrogen and methane.

Windblown plume 150 km long

Plume of nitrogen and dust rises

Geyser vent

Falling dust creates dark streaks on surface

AROUND NEPTUNE

The four innermost moons orbit among the planet's rings, although Thalassa and Naiad do not appear to be acting as "shepherds." Triton, 354,800 km out, is the seventh-largest moon in the Solar System and the only major moon to circle its parent planet backward—perhaps a sign that it was "captured" by Neptune's gravity after a collision with another moon. Distant Nereid was probably captured on a later occasion.

Larissa   Galatea   Despoina   Thalassa   Naiad

Narrow D ring   Broad B ring   Narrow C ring   Broad A ring

4   3   2   1

SCALE IN RADII OF NEPTUNE

Farthest moon: 5.51 million km from Neptune

230   210   15   10   5

Nereid   *Triton*   *Proteus*   *Larissa*

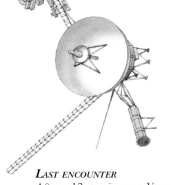

SMALL DARK SPOT
This cloud feature spins in a direction opposite to that of the Great Dark Spot: it is made of descending material. In its center is a region of upwelling cloud.

LAST ENCOUNTER
After a 12-year journey, Voyager 2 flew by Neptune on August 24, 1989. Its signals took more than 4 hours to reach Earth. The final encounter with Triton swung the probe out of the plane of the Solar System, from which it will escape to fly among the stars.

FACTS AND FIGURES

Diameter (equatorial)	49,528 km
Diameter (polar)	48,600 km
Average distance from Sun	4,497,070,000 km
Orbital speed around Sun	5.43 km/sec
Circles Sun (a "year")	164.79 years
A "day"	
Turns on axis	
Sunrise to sunrise }	16 hours 7 minutes
Mass (Earth = 1)	17.14
Average density (water = 1)	1.64
Surface gravity (Earth = 1)	1.12
Temperature at cloud tops	−210°C

ACTIVITIES

● You cannot see Neptune with the naked eye—it is too faint because it is so far from the Sun.

● With binoculars and a chart showing Neptune's current position, try to pick out the planet as it moves gradually against the background stars. It should look like a very faint, bluish "star."

● You will need a moderate-sized telescope to reveal Neptune as a disk and to show its largest moon, Triton.

PLUTO

THE DISCOVERY OF PLUTO marked the end of a search that had lasted for nearly 75 years. Once astronomers discovered Neptune they soon realized that its gravity alone was not strong enough to pull Uranus away from its expected orbit. The hunt for a ninth planet was on. Among the most dedicated of the searchers was an American astronomer, Percival Lowell. He failed, but 12 years after his death his old observatory hired a young astronomer, Clyde Tombaugh, to continue the search. In February 1930, Tombaugh spotted Pluto, the smallest planet of all. It has one moon, Charon, fully half its size. Because the two are so similar in size, they behave like a "double planet" (*see below*). Even their combined gravities, however, would be too small to have any effect on Uranus. So was Pluto the missing world? Or is there a tenth planet still to be discovered?

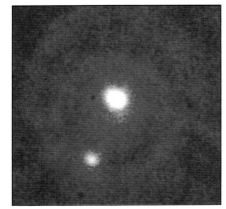

Seeing double: the smallest planet in the Solar System and its moon, Charon, as seen from the orbiting Hubble Space Telescope.

DWARF WORLDS

Both Pluto and Charon spin at an angle of 57.5° from the vertical and in a direction opposite to that of the other planets. Pluto is tiny and insubstantial: Earth is five times larger and 500 times more massive.

Earth

Charon

Pluto

57.5°

57.5°

STRUCTURE / ATMOSPHERE

WATER AND METHANE ICE

WATER ICE

CORE

RADIUS: 1,142 KILOMETERS

METHANE

NITROGEN?

INSIDE PLUTO

Pluto and Charon are not only denser than the gas giants but also denser than the icy moons of Uranus and Neptune. This means they must contain rock. Both probably have large rocky cores covered by icy mantles. When Pluto is closest to the Sun, it develops a very thin atmosphere. This contains methane and, probably, nitrogen.

Eccentric orbit

Pluto has a very unplanetlike orbit—its path around the Sun is very elongated, or elliptical, taking it inside Neptune's orbit for 20 years of its 248-year orbit. And unlike the other planets, whose orbits all lie within a few degrees of one plane, Pluto's is tilted by 17°. Despite its peculiar orbit, however, Pluto is almost certainly a genuine planet—it is too big to be a comet or an asteroid.

LONELY PLANET
Pluto is the only planet not to have been visited by a space probe, but this is an impression of how the surface of the planet and its moon might look. Space scientists would like to mount a mission to Pluto, but the journey would take at least 10–15 years.

CHARON
At 19,640 km, Charon is 20 times closer to Pluto than the Moon is to Earth. Its surface appears to be covered in water ice with no methane present.

Orbit of Pluto

Orbit of Neptune

Orbit of Uranus

WANDERING WORLD
The elliptical and angled orbit of Pluto. In 1979, it passed inside Neptune's orbit, losing its title of the "outermost planet" until 1999. Mercury (too small to be seen here) has the second most unusual orbit, but it is not nearly as elliptical and is tilted by only 7°.

Double planet

Like Earth and the Moon, Pluto and Charon form a "double planet." An American astronomer, Jim Christy, discovered Charon in 1978 after noticing that in some images Pluto looked pear-shaped. He concluded that this odd appearance was because there were two objects—Pluto and a moon—very close together. Charon is 1,192 km across, just over half of Pluto's 2,284 km diameter.

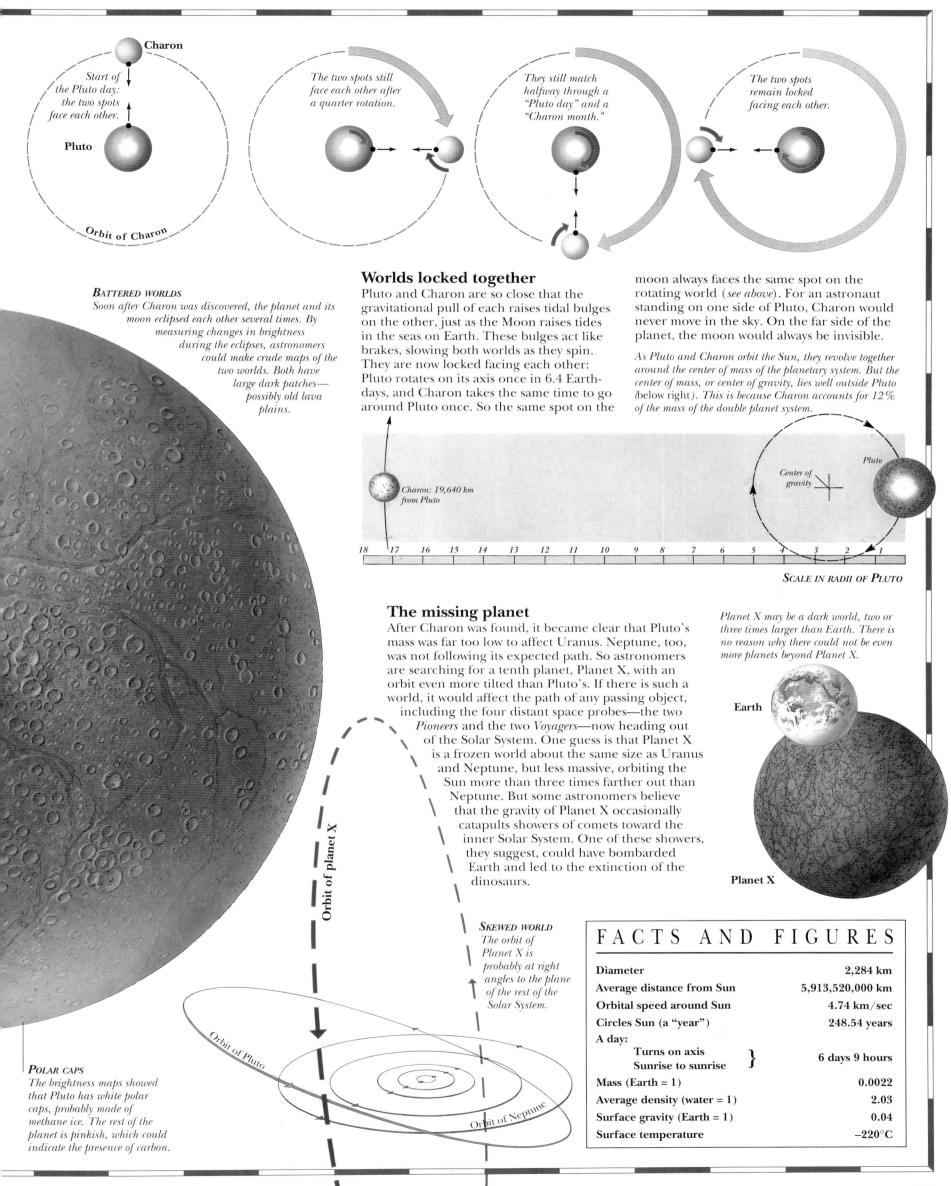

Start of the Pluto day: the two spots face each other.

Charon

Pluto

Orbit of Charon

The two spots still face each other after a quarter rotation.

They still match halfway through a "Pluto day" and a "Charon month."

The two spots remain locked facing each other.

Worlds locked together

Pluto and Charon are so close that the gravitational pull of each raises tidal bulges on the other, just as the Moon raises tides in the seas on Earth. These bulges act like brakes, slowing both worlds as they spin. They are now locked facing each other: Pluto rotates on its axis once in 6.4 Earth-days, and Charon takes the same time to go around Pluto once. So the same spot on the moon always faces the same spot on the rotating world (*see above*). For an astronaut standing on one side of Pluto, Charon would never move in the sky. On the far side of the planet, the moon would always be invisible.

As Pluto and Charon orbit the Sun, they revolve together around the center of mass of the planetary system. But the center of mass, or center of gravity, lies well outside Pluto (below right). This is because Charon accounts for 12% of the mass of the double planet system.

BATTERED WORLDS
Soon after Charon was discovered, the planet and its moon eclipsed each other several times. By measuring changes in brightness during the eclipses, astronomers could make crude maps of the two worlds. Both have large dark patches— possibly old lava plains.

Charon: 19,640 km from Pluto

Center of gravity

Pluto

| 18 | 17 | 16 | 15 | 14 | 13 | 12 | 11 | 10 | 9 | 8 | 7 | 6 | 5 | 4 | 3 | 2 | 1 |

SCALE IN RADII OF PLUTO

The missing planet

After Charon was found, it became clear that Pluto's mass was far too low to affect Uranus. Neptune, too, was not following its expected path. So astronomers are searching for a tenth planet, Planet X, with an orbit even more tilted than Pluto's. If there is such a world, it would affect the path of any passing object, including the four distant space probes—the two *Pioneers* and the two *Voyagers*—now heading out of the Solar System. One guess is that Planet X is a frozen world about the same size as Uranus and Neptune, but less massive, orbiting the Sun more than three times farther out than Neptune. But some astronomers believe that the gravity of Planet X occasionally catapults showers of comets toward the inner Solar System. One of these showers, they suggest, could have bombarded Earth and led to the extinction of the dinosaurs.

Planet X may be a dark world, two or three times larger than Earth. There is no reason why there could not be even more planets beyond Planet X.

Earth

Planet X

Orbit of planet X

SKEWED WORLD
The orbit of Planet X is probably at right angles to the plane of the rest of the Solar System.

Orbit of Pluto

Orbit of Neptune

POLAR CAPS
The brightness maps showed that Pluto has white polar caps, probably made of methane ice. The rest of the planet is pinkish, which could indicate the presence of carbon.

FACTS AND FIGURES

Diameter	2,284 km
Average distance from Sun	5,913,520,000 km
Orbital speed around Sun	4.74 km/sec
Circles Sun (a "year")	248.54 years
A day:	
Turns on axis Sunrise to sunrise	6 days 9 hours
Mass (Earth = 1)	0.0022
Average density (water = 1)	2.03
Surface gravity (Earth = 1)	0.04
Surface temperature	−220°C

COMETS

THE SIGHT OF A GREAT COMET hanging in the sky, looking like a ghostly dagger poised to strike, is an impressive spectacle. Yet comets are all show and no substance—a "dirty snowball" or lump of ice just a few kilometers across leftover from the birth of the Solar System. When the comet's orbit carries it close to the Sun, surface ices evaporate into a great head of steam, which the solar wind sweeps into a long tail. The comet's moment of glory lasts only a few weeks before it heads back to the icy outer reaches of the Solar System. Unfortunately, there have been no truly great comets in recent years. But comets are notoriously unpredictable: they can appear suddenly, as if out of nowhere.

One of the most impressive comets of recent years, Comet West, appeared in 1976. Its two tails are visible here: a straight blue gas tail and a curved yellowish dust tail.

By the time a comet passes Mars, the tail should be developing.

The gas tail is straight: forced back by electrically charged particles in the solar wind.

A COMET'S TAIL

The long, oval orbit of a comet carries it close to the Sun and far away again. As it approaches the Sun, the frozen surface starts to evaporate, forming a great head of gas—the comet's "coma." The solar wind forces back the gas and particles of dust carried away with the evaporating gas into a pair of tails that grow as the comet rounds the Sun. The gas tail may be 100 million kilometers or more long. As the comet recedes, the tail shrinks again.

Even when receding from the Sun, a comet goes "tail first"—because the tail is being pushed back by the solar wind.

The dust tail follows the curve of the comet's path, pushed away by sunlight.

The tail is longest at the closest approach to the Sun, when gas-production is highest.

REGULAR VISITOR

Halley's Comet has visited the inner Solar System every 76 years since at least 240 B.C. It is named after Edmond Halley, a British astronomer. In 1705 he realized that several "different" comets were one and the same object.

GAS   NUCLEUS   DUST

An artist's impression of the nucleus of a comet emitting jets of gas and dust. The gas escaping from the comet is forced back by the solar wind.

Inside a comet

The "naked" comet itself, the nucleus, lies deep inside the coma. Until the *Giotto* space probe flew past Halley's Comet in 1986, no one had seen a comet's nucleus. In Halley, the nucleus is a potato-shaped lump of ice and rock measuring 16 x 8 km and coated with material blacker than coal. It is not smooth, but has low hills and craters. Under the Sun's heat, jets of gas break through the thin crust, and the dust coating the surface streams away into space.

The size of a family car, the European Giotto *probe flew into the heart of Halley's Comet at a speed of 250,000 km/hr. High-speed dust particles from the comet destroyed some of the instruments.*

MISSION TO HALLEY

In March 1986, the *Giotto* probe flew within 600 km of the nucleus of Halley's Comet. As well as sending back images of the heart of the comet, *Giotto* sampled the gases given off (mainly water vapor) and analyzed the dust particles. There are now plans to build a craft to rendezvous with a comet and take samples from the nucleus. This will shed light on the origins of our planets: astronomers believe comets are cosmic debris unchanged since the birth of the Solar System.

Where do comets come from?

No one knows for certain where comets originate. But their long orbits must mean that they come from far beyond the known planets. In 1950, the Dutch astronomer Jan Oort suggested that comets reside in a gigantic cloud that surrounds our Solar System. The inner edge of the "Oort Cloud" may come in as close as the orbit of Neptune, while the outer limits may lie two light years away—halfway to the nearest star. Although astronomers have not directly observed the Oort Cloud, they estimate that it contains a million million million comets in their frozen state, in varying orbits around the Sun. Every so often, the gravity of a passing star can "knock" a comet from its orbit so that it falls toward the Sun. Roughly ten comets a year are newcomers to the inner Solar System, where many—as happened with Halley's Comet—become trapped. Astronomers think the Oort Cloud is the remains of the nebula that formed the Sun and planets; if so, comets can tell us about what conditions were like when the Solar System was born.

HALLEY'S DECLINE
Every time Halley's Comet revisits, it loses up to 250 million tonnes of material. At this rate, it will last another 170,000 years.

Outer cloud

Inner cloud

STRUCTURE OF THE OORT CLOUD
Many comets may be concentrated in an "inner cloud," orbiting the Sun in much the same plane as the planets (shown, inset, magnified 1,000 times). The comets in the "outer cloud" may be scattered into random orbits by passing stars. The dark region between the two clouds contains relatively few comets.

Orbit of Neptune

Orbit of Pluto

WHAT KIND OF COMET?

Comets are classed roughly into three types. Nonperiodic comets are those whose orbits are so large that they take millions of years to orbit the Sun—Delavan's Comet of 1914, for example, will not be seen again in our part of the Solar System for an estimated 24 million years. Long-period comets take more than 200 years to complete an orbit—sometimes thousands of years. Short-period comets are those trapped by the gravity of the planets, particularly Jupiter, and orbit the Sun relatively quickly. The comet with the shortest period, Comet Encke, takes 3.3 years to orbit the Sun.

KOPFF
This long-period comet made its first visit to the Sun in 1905 when a small piece of the nucleus broke off. It will not appear again for thousands of years.

KLEMOLA
First seen in 1965 from Argentina, Comet Klemola orbits the Sun every 11 years.

STEPHAN-OTERMA
A short-period comet seen passing close to the Sun in 1867, 1942, and 1980. Next due in 2018?

HALLEY
Orbiting the Sun every 76 years, Halley has passed by Earth 30 times since 240 B.C.

Orbit of Uranus

Orbit of Neptune

Orbit of Pluto

A long-exposure photograph captures a meteor (the long streak on the right; the short streaks are trails of stars) from the Geminid shower. The meteors appear to radiate from the constellation of Gemini.

Shooting stars

Comets leave a trail of material behind as they travel the Solar System. Several times a year, Earth plows into the debris—particles of dust—strewn along comets' orbits. The dust particles stream into our atmosphere by the million but, because they are small and light, they burn up harmlessly as a display of meteors, or shooting stars. Debris is spread out along the orbit of a periodic comet, producing an annual shower of meteors as Earth crosses the orbit.

METEOR SHOWERS

Shower	Date of maximum activity	Maximum number per hour
Quadrantids	January 3–4	50
Lyrids	April 22	10
Eta Aquarids	May 5	10
Delta Aquarids	July 31	25
Perseids	August 12	50
Orionids	October 21	20
Taurids	November 8	10
Leonids	November 17	10
Geminids	December 14	50
Ursids	December 22	15

The main meteor showers visible during the year. Of these, the Perseids give the most spectacular show.

ACTIVITIES

● Most comets are very faint, and you will need a telescope or binoculars to see them. Occasionally, though, a brilliant comet appears unexpectedly.

● Some astronomers specialize in hunting down comets. It is a difficult task, but if you discover a comet, it is named after you!

● Look for news of comets in the newspapers or on TV—then go to the darkest place you know of for the best chance of spotting the comet.

● You can spot bits of worn-out comets—meteors—as they fall into the atmosphere and burn up. And you will not need a telescope—your eye is the best instrument for the job.

OUR LOCAL STAR

THE SUN IS OUR LOCAL STAR. Like most stars, the Sun is an immense globe of glowing hydrogen gas. The hydrogen at the heart of the globe, lying under the huge weight of the outer layers, is so hot and compressed that hydrogen atoms fuse to make helium. In effect, the core of the Sun is a gigantic hydrogen bomb: but the weight of its outer layers stops the reaction from running out of control. That is the difference between a planet and a star: stars have "fusion reactors" to make them shine while planets do not. The Sun's nuclear energy, in the form of light and heat, has bathed the Solar System for 5 billion years, while its enormous gravity has kept the planets in their orbits. All life on Earth is dependent on our local star.

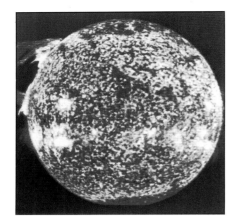

The outer layers of the Sun, photographed from the Skylab Space Station in 1973.

CHROMOSPHERE

PHOTOSPHERE

CONVECTIVE ZONE

RADIATIVE ZONE

INSIDE THE SUN

At the core, the temperature is 14 million degrees: hot enough for energy-generating nuclear reactions to take place. The energy floods outward by radiation. On reaching the convective zone, it is carried upward by the Sun's gases, which rise and fall in huge bubbles. Finally, the energy emerges at the surface, the photosphere, as light and heat. The temperature here is a mere 5,500°C— still hot enough to vaporize every substance we know. Above the photosphere lies the atmosphere, which is divided into the chromosphere and the corona extending to Pluto and beyond.

CORE

HANGERS-ON
Prominences extend hundreds of thousands of kilometers into the corona. Many are associated with sunspots, where magnetic fields force the red-hot gas into giant arches. Most prominences hang from the chromosphere for months, but sometimes one will blast off into space.

COOL SPOTS
There is usually a scattering of sunspots—regions of gas that look darker because they are cooler. They are caused by the Sun's magnetic field.

The solar wind not only blows a magnetic bubble, the heliosphere, but also generates electric currents. The currents flow in a huge thin sheet which flutters and sways like a ballerina's skirt as the Sun rotates.

OUTER EDGE OF HELIOSPHERE

INTERSTELLAR GASES

Pluto   Sun

CURRENT SHEET

Cosmic Radiation

INTERSTELLAR GASES

The gas filling the heliosphere is very hot (100,000°C) but so thin that it does not vaporize spacecraft!

FAST RISERS
Small straight jets of gas, spicules, shoot to a height of 10,000 km, and then fall back after a few minutes. Spicules appear to be associated with strong magnetic fields.

Solar bubble

The Sun's influence extends to the very edge of the Solar System. Its corona feeds fast-moving gas into the "solar wind," a gale of charged particles such as protons and electrons that rush away from the Sun at speeds of up to 3 million km/hr. These particles generate magnetic fields and electric currents, which fill the apparently empty space in the Solar System. The planets all orbit inside this magnetic environment, the heliosphere. It acts as a protective bubble, cocooning the Sun's family of planets from the cosmic radiation that exists between the stars.

UNEVEN ROTATION
Sunspots change their positions on the disk because of the Sun's uneven rotation—it spins faster at the equator than at the poles.

Sunspots

Strong magnetic fields sometimes "dam" the flow of heat from the Sun's interior to the photosphere. Even so, the temperature of these cooler regions, known as sunspots, is about 4,000°C. Sunspots appear in pairs, one at each end of the loop of the magnetic field. In the cross-section below, you can see how the cool region extends below the photosphere. Some sunspots grow as large as Jupiter and last for months. Others may grow to only a few hundred kilometers and disappear after a day or two.

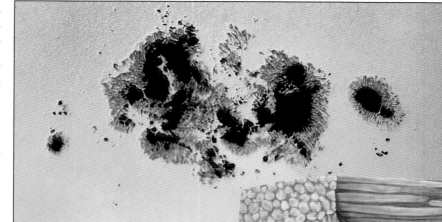

THE SOLAR CYCLE

The number of sunspots changes over a cycle of about 11 years. The first spots of a new cycle appear near the poles. Over the next few years, spots appear in increasing numbers, closer and closer to the equator, until reaching solar maximum. The cycle is probably caused by the Sun's uneven rotation pushing bands of magnetic activity toward the equator. The next solar maximum is due in about 2001.

Penumbra: the outer part of the sunspot

Umbra: the darkest and coolest part of a sunspot

Photosphere: the bubbles, or granules, are where heat rises to the surface by convection

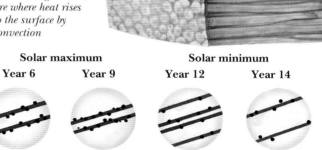

Solar minimum		Solar maximum		Solar minimum	
Year 1	Year 3	Year 6	Year 9	Year 12	Year 14

At the Sun's core

Every second, the Sun converts 4 million tonnes of itself into energy. Its source of apparently limitless power is the nuclear fusion of hydrogen that takes place at the core. A proton (the nucleus of a hydrogen atom) fuses with another proton to make deuterium (consisting of a proton and an electrically neutral particle, a neutron). Further protons combine with this to make helium-3 (two protons and one neutron), which react in pairs to form helium-4 (two protons and two neutrons). In each reaction, a little mass is lost—and this is turned into the Sun's energy. Although the energy starts as a searing blast of gamma rays, it ends up being given off as light and heat after working its way to the surface.

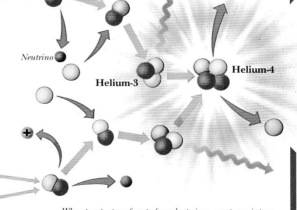

When two protons fuse to form deuterium, one turns into a neutron and releases two lightweight particles: a positively charged positron and an electrically neutral neutrino.

ULYSSES
Although we can easily see the regions around the Sun's equator, we have never seen its poles. In 1994–95, however, the Ulysses satellite will fly over the Sun's poles—at a safe distance—and send back data on what conditions are like there. It will tell scientists a lot about the Sun's magnetic field.

FACTS AND FIGURES

Age	4.5 billion years
Diameter	1.4 million km
Distance from Earth	149.6 million km
Distance to nearest star	9.46 million million km
Rotation period at equator	25 Earth days
Rotation period at poles	35 Earth days
Mass (Earth = 1)	330,000
Density (water = 1)	1.41
Temperature at surface	5,500°C
Temperature at core	14,000,000°C
Luminosity	390 billion billion megawatts

ACTIVITIES

● **NEVER** look at the Sun directly, and **absolutely NEVER** with a telescope or binoculars. The concentrated heat and light could blind you.

● Ask an expert to show you how to **safely** use a telescope to project an image of the Sun onto a piece of white paper. Then you can view the sunspots.

● Make a simple sundial by putting a straight stick into soft ground, and mark the positions of its shadow at sunrise, noon, and sunset.

NEAREST STARS

IF IT WERE POSSIBLE TO TRAVEL to the Sun by jet plane, the journey would take you two years. If you were to catch the same jet to the nearest star, Proxima Centauri, the trip would last 5 million years. Even nearby stars are a very, very long way away: Proxima Centauri is 40 million million kilometers distant. Star distances, when described in kilometers, give impossibly big numbers. Instead, astronomers refer to the time it takes for a star's light to reach Earth. In the vacuum of space, light always travels at the same speed—at the speed limit of the Universe. In one second, a ray of light travels nearly 300,000 kilometers. It takes 8.3 minutes for light to reach us from the Sun, and so we say the Sun is 8.3 light-minutes away. Pluto, at the edge of the Solar System, lies about 5 light-hours away. Proxima Centauri is 4.2 light-years distant. A light-year is equivalent to 9.5 million million kilometers.

NEAREST OF ALL
Proxima is part of Alpha Centauri, a triple-star system in the constellation of Centaurus. The two main stars are like the Sun, but dim red Proxima is only visible with a powerful telescope.

FROM BRIGHT TO DIM

Just over 2,000 years ago, the Greek astronomer Hipparchus devised a way of measuring the apparent magnitude of stars— how bright they appear in the sky. He divided them into six classes of magnitude. Each class was about 2 1/2 times brighter than the next, making first magnitude stars about a hundred times brighter than those of magnitude 6. We use the same system today but have extended it to include brighter and fainter stars. Brilliant stars have magnitudes of zero or even negative numbers (Sirius, the brightest star in the sky, is magnitude –1.5). And powerful telescopes can detect stars of magnitude 26, nearly 100 billion times fainter than Sirius. To measure the actual, or "absolute" brightness of a star, you need to know how far away it is.

−1
0
1
2
3
4
5
6
7

OTHER SOLAR SYSTEMS

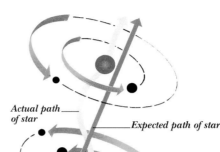

Vega is one star that is surrounded by rings of dust, which may be the "building blocks" of planets. Do other stars have planets? We don't know: stars are large and luminous and any planets would be too small, dark, and close in for us to see.

SEARCHING FOR NEW WORLDS

Even if you cannot see planets around stars, there are ways of finding them. One way is to look for "wobbles" in the path of nearby stars. If a massive planet were orbiting a star, the planet's gravity would affect the star's path through space: instead of traveling in a straight line, its path would be wavy. It takes many years of following a star's motion, however, to see the effect. Barnard's Star, 5.9 light-years away, may have a system of planets.

Actual path of star

Expected path of star

Planet 2

Barnard's Star

Planet 1

Some astronomers believe two planets, similar in mass to Jupiter and Saturn, are pulling Barnard's Star out of position.

How far is that star?

Once you know a star's distance, you can measure many of its properties—for instance, brightness and size. Stars are so far away, however, that astronomers tried for many centuries before they succeeded in measuring the distance to one, using the parallax method (*see below*). Unfortunately, parallax becomes inaccurate for stars more than 300 light-years away, which doesn't get us very far in a Galaxy 100,000 light-years across. For more distant stars, astronomers have to resort to other tactics. These include watching stars in a cluster and measuring how they move; measuring how much a star appears fainter—because of distance—than a nearby star of the same type; and monitoring how some very brilliant stars change in brightness.

SURVEYING SPACE

A star appears to shift its position against the background of more distant stars if viewed from opposite sides of Earth's orbit. From the size of this parallax shift and the diameter of Earth's orbit, astronomers can calculate the star's distance. The farther the star, the smaller the shift.

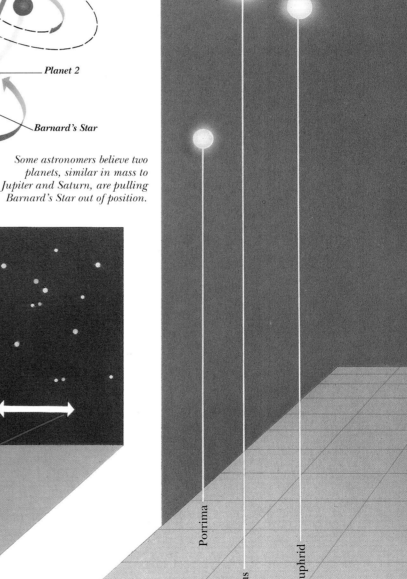

STAR B

STAR A

Earth in January

SUN

Earth in July

Porrima

Arcturus

Muphrid

Our celestial neighborhood

Many of the stars within 40 light-years of the Sun are small, dim, red stars. These red dwarfs are the most common stars in our Galaxy, even though we are usually unaware of them because they are hard to pick out at great distances. Some of the Sun's neighbors are more impressive: for example, the triple-star system Alpha Centauri; Sirius, the brightest star in the sky; orange-red Arcturus; dazzling white Vega; and yellow Capella. Although the nearby stars seem widely scattered through space, they occupy only a very small region of one of the several arms of stars that make up our spiral Galaxy.

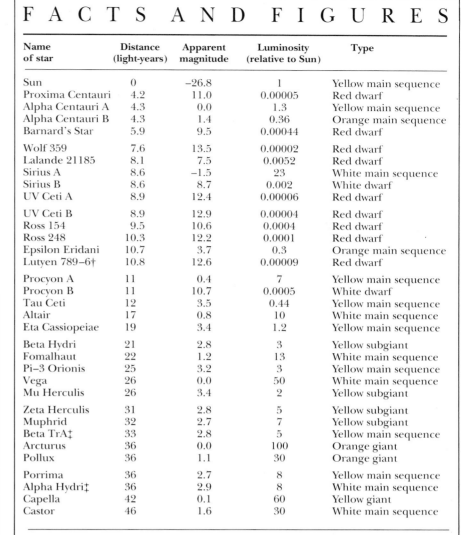

FACTS AND FIGURES

Name of star	Distance (light-years)	Apparent magnitude	Luminosity (relative to Sun)	Type
Sun	0	−26.8	1	Yellow main sequence
Proxima Centauri	4.2	11.0	0.00005	Red dwarf
Alpha Centauri A	4.3	0.0	1.3	Yellow main sequence
Alpha Centauri B	4.3	1.4	0.36	Orange main sequence
Barnard's Star	5.9	9.5	0.00044	Red dwarf
Wolf 359	7.6	13.5	0.00002	Red dwarf
Lalande 21185	8.1	7.5	0.0052	Red dwarf
Sirius A	8.6	−1.5	23	White main sequence
Sirius B	8.6	8.7	0.002	White dwarf
UV Ceti A	8.9	12.4	0.00006	Red dwarf
UV Ceti B	8.9	12.9	0.00004	Red dwarf
Ross 154	9.5	10.6	0.0004	Red dwarf
Ross 248	10.3	12.2	0.0001	Red dwarf
Epsilon Eridani	10.7	3.7	0.3	Orange main sequence
Lutyen 789–6†	10.8	12.6	0.00009	Red dwarf
Procyon A	11	0.4	7	Yellow main sequence
Procyon B	11	10.7	0.0005	White dwarf
Tau Ceti	12	3.5	0.44	Yellow main sequence
Altair	17	0.8	10	White main sequence
Eta Cassiopeiae	19	3.4	1.2	Yellow main sequence
Beta Hydri	21	2.8	3	Yellow subgiant
Fomalhaut	22	1.2	13	White main sequence
Pi–3 Orionis	25	3.2	3	Yellow main sequence
Vega	26	0.0	50	White main sequence
Mu Herculis	26	3.4	2	Yellow subgiant
Zeta Herculis	31	2.8	5	Yellow subgiant
Muphrid	32	2.7	7	Yellow subgiant
Beta TrA‡	33	2.8	5	Yellow main sequence
Arcturus	36	0.0	100	Orange giant
Pollux	36	1.1	30	Orange giant
Porrima	36	2.7	8	Yellow main sequence
Alpha Hydri‡	36	2.9	8	White main sequence
Capella	42	0.1	60	Yellow giant
Castor	46	1.6	30	White main sequence

† After Lutyen 789–6, the table does not include any of the dozens of red dwarfs.
‡ These stars fall just outside the area of our Galaxy that this map covers.

THE DOG AND THE PUP
Sirius, or the Dog Star, outshines all the other stars in the sky, but only because it is so close (8.6 light-years). Some stars are a million times more luminous but appear fainter because they are so far away. Sirius has a companion: a tiny star of magnitude 8 nicknamed the Pup. This is a white dwarf—the dying remnant of a star like Sirius.

Labels (on diagram, left to right): Castor · Pollux · Lalande 21185 · Barnard's Star · Wolf 359 · Procyon · Sirius · Alpha Centauri · **Sun** · Ross 154 · Beta Hydri · Capella · Pi–3 Orionis · Epsilon Eridani · Ross 248 · UV Ceti · Altair · Lutyen 789–6 · Tau Ceti · Eta Cassiopeiae · Fomalhaut · Zeta Herculis · Vega · Mu Herculis

ACTIVITIES

● See how many of the nearby stars you can find in the sky. Remember when you look at Vega (which is 26 light-years away) that although neighboring Deneb may look as bright, it is a superluminous star that is 1,800 light-years away.

● If you have access to a good telescope (that is, one with a mirror more than 20 cm across), see if you can spot Sirius's faint companion.

● Try the parallax method for yourself. Hold one finger about 15 centimeters in front of your face, and see how it seems to jump as you look at it first with one eye, then the other. Now move the finger to arm's length: the jump is much smaller.

STARS OF NORTHERN SKIES

THE STARS ARE ALL VERY FAR APART. But from Earth it looks as if they are stuck on the inside of a bowl, all at the same distance, and arranged into groups and patterns—the constellations. Each culture has invented its own constellations, and many of the ones we know today are ones that the Babylonians and Greeks used more than 2,500 years ago. Our ancestors relied on star patterns to tell the time: the stars rise and set as Earth spins. They used stars to navigate by: Polaris lies almost exactly above Earth's North Pole. The constellations even provided a calendar: we see different star patterns from month to month as Earth orbits the Sun. Constellations are not real groups of stars—the stars in them are not associated with each other—but they are an excellent way to locate and identify different stars.

How to use this star map

This map is for stargazing north of the equator. Find the current month around the edge of the map, and turn the book until this month is at the bottom. Face south at night and look for the stars as they appear on the map—you should be able to see most of the stars shown in the center and lower part of the chart. The map also shows the system of coordinates that astronomers use: declination, measured in degrees, and right ascension, measured in hours (*see page 49*).

ORION
One of the brightest constellations in the sky, Orion was a boastful hunter in the Greek legends. There are many myths associated with him. One is that the gods were tired of Orion's bragging and sent a scorpion to kill him by biting his ankle. Afterward they relented, and placed Orion in the sky for eternity, with the scorpion safely on the opposite side of the sky (see Scorpius, on page 48). Orion contains many brilliant stars, including blood-red Betelgeuse and blue-white Rigel. It is also home to the Orion Nebula, a giant cloud of gas in which new stars are forming.

STARGAZING
The best time of year to start stargazing if you live north of the equator is in winter. Then the brilliant constellation of Orion rises high and you can use it as a signpost to the other constellations.

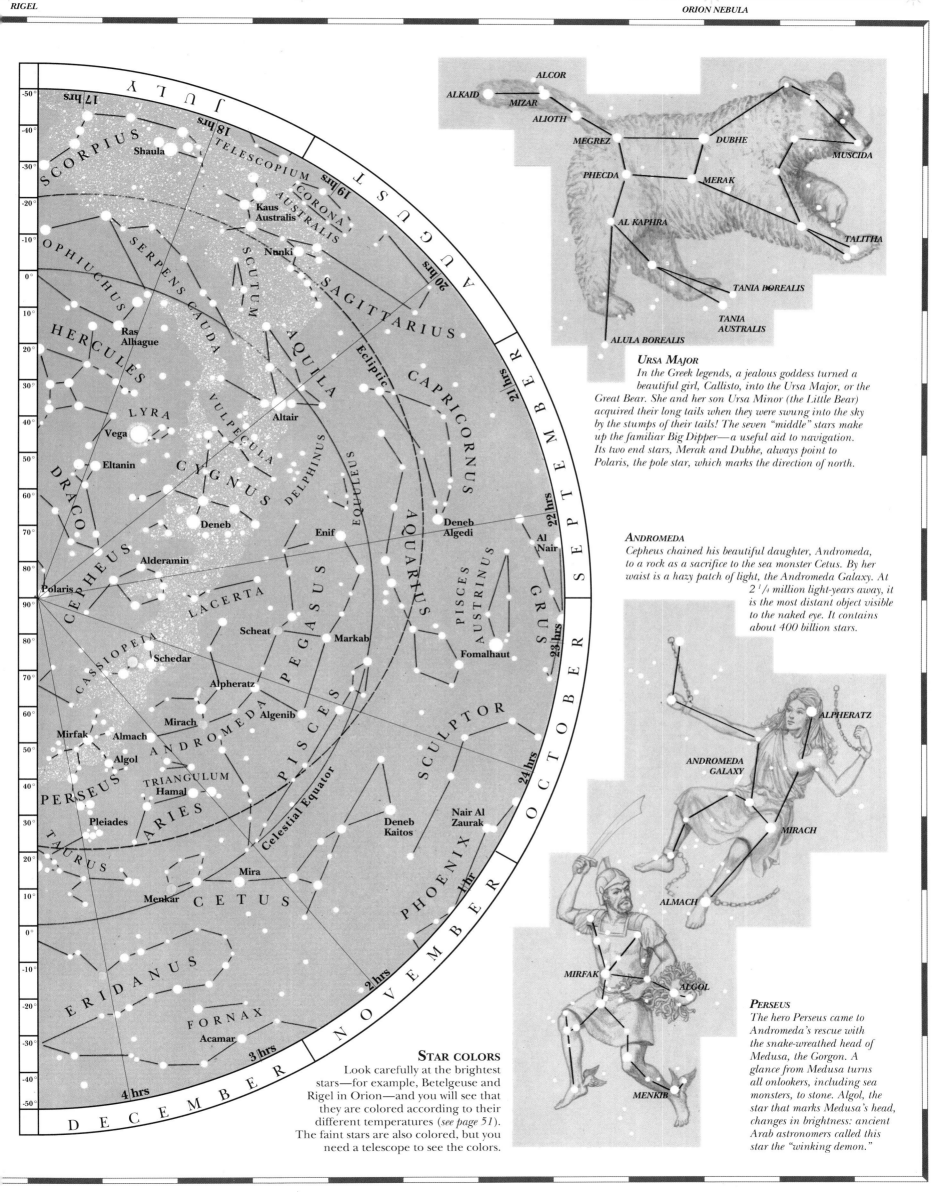

URSA MAJOR

In the Greek legends, a jealous goddess turned a beautiful girl, Callisto, into the Ursa Major, or the Great Bear. She and her son Ursa Minor (the Little Bear) acquired their long tails when they were swung into the sky by the stumps of their tails! The seven "middle" stars make up the familiar Big Dipper—a useful aid to navigation. Its two end stars, Merak and Dubhe, always point to Polaris, the pole star, which marks the direction of north.

ANDROMEDA

Cepheus chained his beautiful daughter, Andromeda, to a rock as a sacrifice to the sea monster Cetus. By her waist is a hazy patch of light, the Andromeda Galaxy. At 2 1/4 million light-years away, it is the most distant object visible to the naked eye. It contains about 400 billion stars.

PERSEUS

The hero Perseus came to Andromeda's rescue with the snake-wreathed head of Medusa, the Gorgon. A glance from Medusa turns all onlookers, including sea monsters, to stone. Algol, the star that marks Medusa's head, changes in brightness: ancient Arab astronomers called this star the "winking demon."

STAR COLORS

Look carefully at the brightest stars—for example, Betelgeuse and Rigel in Orion—and you will see that they are colored according to their different temperatures (see page 51). The faint stars are also colored, but you need a telescope to see the colors.

47

STARS OF SOUTHERN SKIES

THE FIRST EUROPEANS TO OBSERVE THE STARS south of the equator were the explorers of the 17th and 18th centuries. They set their seal on the southern sky, using names that were familiar to them—such as Pictor (the painter), Antlia (the air pump), and Indus (the Indian)—for the constellations that are never visible in the north. The southern hemisphere does not have the north's pole star to help navigators, but its skies are undeniably more spectacular. This part of the globe faces the center of our Galaxy, looking out onto the densest concentrations of bright stars. You can also see the two nearest galaxies, the Large and Small Magellanic Clouds.

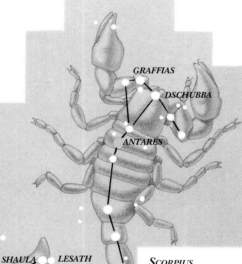

SCORPIUS
This is one of the few constellations that looks like its namesake, the scorpion. Scorpius was the creature who defeated Orion (see page 46). A brilliant red star, Antares, or "rival of Mars," marks the "heart" of Scorpius. Antares is 300 times larger than our Sun and is so vast that it cannot control its outer layers: it changes in brightness as it swells and shrinks.

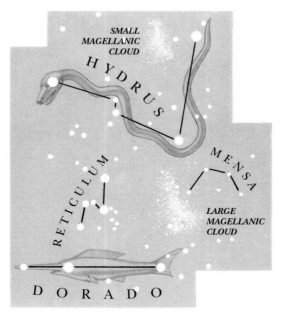

MAGELLANIC CLOUDS
Our Galaxy's two closest neighbors, the Large and Small Magellanic Clouds, are easily visible to the naked eye. They may look like patches from our own Milky Way that have become detached but in fact they are more than 150,000 light-years away. Both galaxies contain hundreds of millions of stars and are much smaller than our Galaxy. In 1987, one of the stars in the Large Cloud exploded: the first supernova to be visible to the naked eye in 383 years.

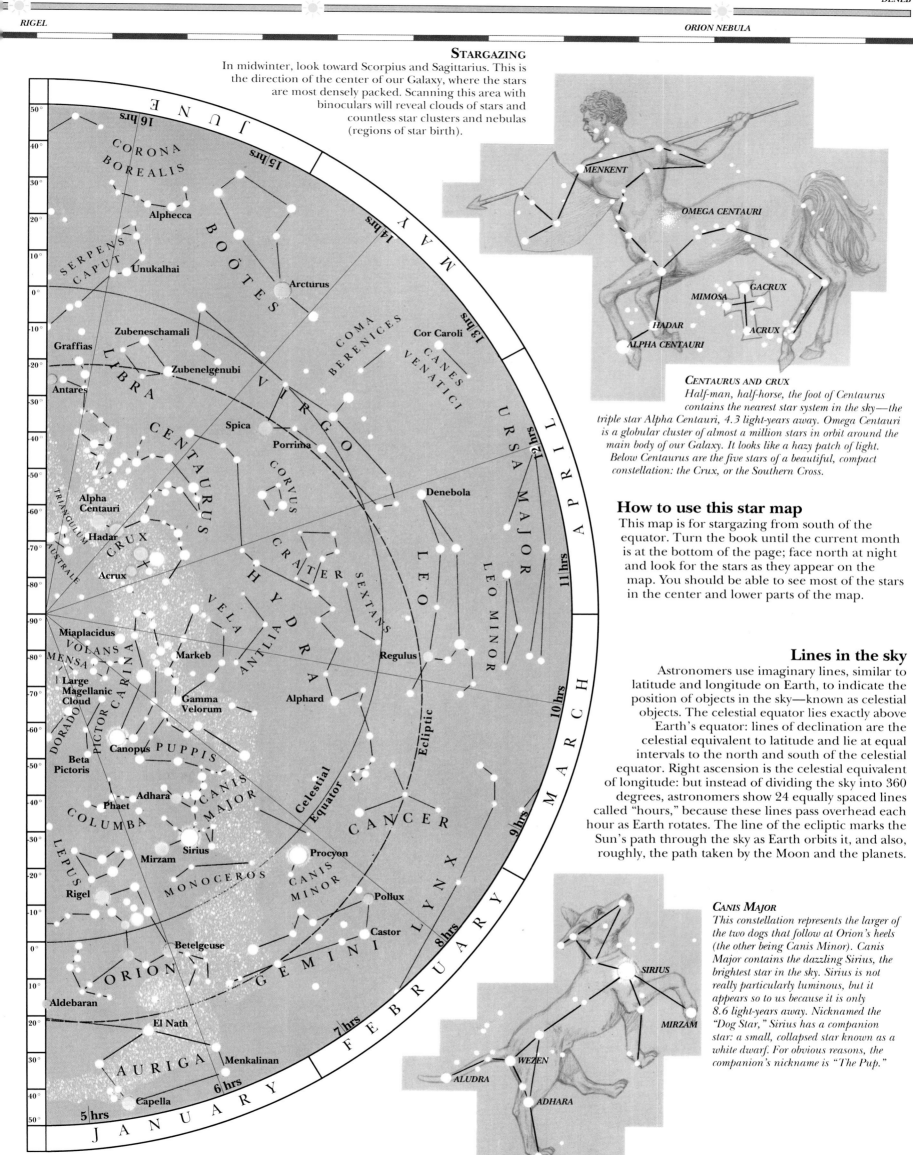

STARGAZING

In midwinter, look toward Scorpius and Sagittarius. This is the direction of the center of our Galaxy, where the stars are most densely packed. Scanning this area with binoculars will reveal clouds of stars and countless star clusters and nebulas (regions of star birth).

CENTAURUS AND CRUX

Half-man, half-horse, the foot of Centaurus contains the nearest star system in the sky—the triple star Alpha Centauri, 4.3 light-years away. Omega Centauri is a globular cluster of almost a million stars in orbit around the main body of our Galaxy. It looks like a hazy patch of light. Below Centaurus are the five stars of a beautiful, compact constellation: the Crux, or the Southern Cross.

How to use this star map

This map is for stargazing from south of the equator. Turn the book until the current month is at the bottom of the page; face north at night and look for the stars as they appear on the map. You should be able to see most of the stars in the center and lower parts of the map.

Lines in the sky

Astronomers use imaginary lines, similar to latitude and longitude on Earth, to indicate the position of objects in the sky—known as celestial objects. The celestial equator lies exactly above Earth's equator: lines of declination are the celestial equivalent to latitude and lie at equal intervals to the north and south of the celestial equator. Right ascension is the celestial equivalent of longitude: but instead of dividing the sky into 360 degrees, astronomers show 24 equally spaced lines called "hours," because these lines pass overhead each hour as Earth rotates. The line of the ecliptic marks the Sun's path through the sky as Earth orbits it, and also, roughly, the path taken by the Moon and the planets.

CANIS MAJOR

This constellation represents the larger of the two dogs that follow at Orion's heels (the other being Canis Minor). Canis Major contains the dazzling Sirius, the brightest star in the sky. Sirius is not really particularly luminous, but it appears so to us because it is only 8.6 light-years away. Nicknamed the "Dog Star," Sirius has a companion star: a small, collapsed star known as a white dwarf. For obvious reasons, the companion's nickname is "The Pup."

BIRTH AND LIFE OF A STAR

ALL STARS HAVE A DEFINITE LIFETIME: they are born, they live, and they die. Their lives are so long, however, that we rarely see a star change as it grows older. But there are so many stars in our Galaxy that we can piece together a life cycle—just as we could guess about how humans age by seeing a snapshot of a crowd of people. The most mysterious part of a star's life is its birth, which takes place deep inside dark clouds of dust and gas known as nebulas. These are so murky that light cannot penetrate, and even powerful telescopes cannot see what is going on. In recent years, however, astronomers have begun using special instruments—infrared detectors—that are sensitive to the heat that is released when stars begin to form. Now we can unravel the secrets of star birth.

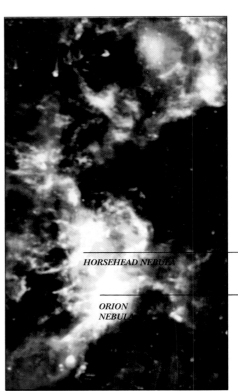

HORSEHEAD NEBULA

ORION NEBULA

Snapshots of star birth

New telescopes have allowed astronomers to understand the sequence of events that changes a dark cloud of gas and dust into a bright, shining star.

❶ WAITING IN THE WINGS
Looking like a chess piece, the Horsehead Nebula (left) is a gigantic dark cloud that will form stars. After a dense cloud (below left) starts to collapse, gravity pulls more and more of the material into the center of the cloud.

❷ HIDDEN FIRES
The dense matter breaks into hundreds of clumps—protostars. The protostars begin to heat up the middle of the cloud—the source of the heat that infrared detectors pick up.

An infrared camera reveals the presence of hot gas where stars are beginning to form in Orion (above). The dark clouds of the Orion and Horsehead Nebulas, in particular, seem to glow with heat.

❸ GOING SOLO
Each protostar continues to shrink independently, becoming denser and denser. It is surrounded by a sphere of dust and gas, which flattens into a disk as the protostar spins.

A star is born

Once a cloud has started to collapse, it will break into hundreds of dense clumps of gas, each of which contracts further. The compression makes the gas in the clumps grow hotter and hotter. Eventually, a clump begins to glow and is called a protostar. It is not an actual star until its nuclear reactions begin, and it starts generating energy. This energy floods out of the clutch of young stars in the form of ultraviolet light, lighting up the wisps of the surrounding cloud so that it glows as a beautiful nebula, such as the famous fan-shaped Orion Nebula (*left*).

Stardust

By earthly standards, the space between the stars is a vacuum. But in reality it contains a very fine sprinkling of atoms of gas and dust (a kind of "soot" from cool, dying stars). Over billions of years, these atoms slowly clump together into gigantic dark clouds hundreds of light-years across. Once a cloud reaches a certain mass, it may start to collapse—perhaps pushed by the force from an exploding star nearby. A collapsing cloud is the first step on the road to star birth. Soon gravity will start to pull the gas and dust into a dense, spinning ball.

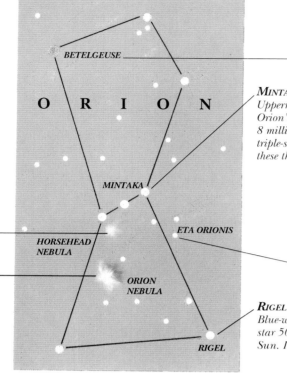

BETELGEUSE
Closer than the other stars in Orion, Betelgeuse is a 10-million-year-old "red giant" near the end of its life. Its red color is visible to the naked eye.

MINTAKA
Uppermost of the three stars in Orion's belt, Mintaka was born 8 million years ago. It is actually a triple-star system: the brightest of these three is a blue-white giant star.

ETA ORIONIS
The brightest member of this triple-star system is a 2-million-year-old main sequence star, some 20 times more massive than the Sun. It is a blue-white star, and shines 1,500 times more brightly than the Sun.

RIGEL
Blue-white Rigel is a superluminous star 50,000 times brighter than the Sun. It is about 5 million years old.

Orion: showcase of star birth

In most constellations, the stars just happen to lie in the same direction in space. The stars in Orion, however, really are associated with one another. Except for Betelgeuse, they are all part of a huge star-forming region: a gigantic bubble in space where young stars are mixed with dark material that has yet to collapse. Dust and gas fill the whole of the Orion region. These are invisible to the naked eye, but easily detected with an infrared camera (*see photograph opposite*). The most obvious sign that star-formation is going on is the Orion Nebula, a fan-shaped cloud of gas 15 light-years across. The stars within the nebula are young—just half a million years old—while other stars, hidden inside dense clouds, are still being born. In the future, the stars forming in the Horsehead Nebula will change it from a dark cloud into a brilliantly glowing nebula, while the stars in the Orion Nebula will slowly drift apart and disperse into space.

YOUNG STARS
Stars live for such a long time that astronomers call a star young until it is several million years old.

❹ STARSHINE
The young star "turns on" its nuclear furnace and produces gas that escapes in the form of a violent stellar wind, channeled into two beams by the surrounding disk.

❺ STELLAR WIND
The force of the stellar wind blows away most of the surrounding cloud of dust and gas. The material in the disk starts to condense.

❻ A GROWING FAMILY
The material in the disk may, as in the case of the young Sun, condense into a family of planets. Otherwise, the stellar wind sweeps it away into space.

❼ SET FOR LIFE
The star is now shining steadily and is on the "main sequence." It will remain virtually unchanged for many millions of years.

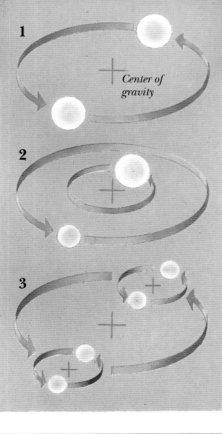

SEEING DOUBLE

Our Sun is a slightly unusual star in that it is all by itself. Sixty percent of stars are actually systems of two or more—for example, Mintaka (in Orion) consists of three stars while Castor (in Gemini) has six. It is not surprising that there are so many double stars, which are called binaries. Stars form in tight, close-knit groups and many stay paired because of the force of each other's gravity. Binaries orbit around each other. The masses of the stars in the system determine the position of the balance point, or center of gravity, of the system, and how the two will orbit each other.

1. *Two stars of equal mass: the balance point of the system lies in the middle.*

2. *One star much more massive than the other: the balance point of the system lies closer to the center of the heavier star.*

3. *In a double-double system: each star orbits its companion, and the two pairs orbit a common balance point.*

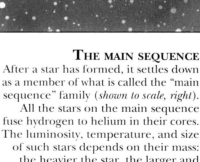

Center of gravity

THE MAIN SEQUENCE

After a star has formed, it settles down as a member of what is called the "main sequence" family (*shown to scale, right*).

All the stars on the main sequence fuse hydrogen to helium in their cores. The luminosity, temperature, and size of such stars depends on their mass: the heavier the star, the larger and hotter it is, and the brighter it shines. Our Sun is a typical main sequence star of average brightness and temperature. More massive stars are bigger, brighter, and hotter: they glow white or blue-white. Stars less massive are smaller, dimmer, and cooler: they glow orange or even red. The so-called brown dwarfs are very cool stars whose mass is not great enough to trigger the nuclear reactions that make stars shine. A star's mass also determines how long it lives: massive stars use up their hydrogen more quickly than stars like the Sun. Less massive stars live longer.

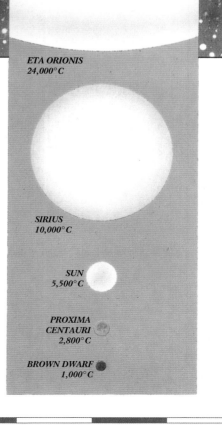

ETA ORIONIS
24,000°C

SIRIUS
10,000°C

SUN
5,500°C

PROXIMA CENTAURI
2,800°C

BROWN DWARF
1,000°C

OLD AGE AND DEATH

STARS LIVE A LONG TIME, but they all die eventually. The reason is simple: they run out of fuel. But the way a star dies, and how long it lives, depends on how massive it is. A star like the Sun, or one that is less massive, lives for billions of years. When its central core runs out of fuel—hydrogen gas—the star swells and becomes a red giant. Eventually, the outer layers drift off into space, leaving the dead core—known as a white dwarf. A white dwarf has no fuel, and its heat slowly leaks away into space. As it cools, it grows steadily dimmer, fading from white to yellow, orange, and then red before finishing life as a cold, black globe. Massive stars, however, go out with a bang, not a whimper. After a short lifetime of a few million years, a heavy star explodes as a supernova, scattering its innards into space. Amazingly, its core may survive as a neutron star, or even as a black hole. But supernovas are not all doom and destruction. Their "ashes" spread out through space and become the raw material for the next generation of stars.

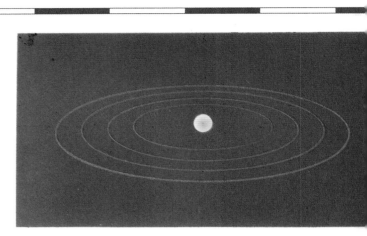

Middle-age spread

Born 4.6 billion years ago, our Sun is now approaching middle age. But it won't change in any dramatic way until it is about 10 billion years old. That is when it will exhaust all the hydrogen supplies in its "nuclear reactor," leaving it with a core made of helium. At this stage, the reactor shuts down. With no energy flowing out of the core, gravity squeezes the core inward, and it grows hotter. This extra heat makes the Sun's outer layers expand toward the orbits of the four innermost planets. The Sun becomes a red giant.

❽ COUNTDOWN TO DOOM
A star more than 10 times heavier than the Sun speeds through its nuclear fuel, shining blue-white, exhausting its supply of hydrogen in just a few million years. As it runs out of hydrogen, it begins to swell.

❾ HOLDING ON . . .
The star has enough gravitational "squeezing power" in the core to fuse helium atoms into carbon. Meanwhile, the extended outer layers have cooled and glow red: the star is now a red giant.

❿ . . . AND ON
When a massive star has "burned" all its helium, it squeezes its core again—forcing the fusion of carbon. This red giant generates energy by fusing successively heavier elements until it has a core of iron.

Crab's beating heart

In 1054, astronomers in China saw a star in the constellation of Taurus explode. Its place today is occupied by a twisted star-wreck 15 light-years across, the Crab Nebula. It is much brighter than the remains of most super-novas. This is because the star left behind an active and kicking corpse: a spinning neutron star, known as a pulsar, which energizes the nebula. The pulsar is only 25 km across, yet it has a mass greater than our Sun. It flashes, or pulses, 30 times a second with astonishing precision. But as time goes by, it is pulsing less rapidly because its spin is slowing down. In a few million years, it will stop pulsing and become a "conventional" neutron star. Astronomers have discovered more than 400 pulsars in our Galaxy; one pulses at 642 times a second.

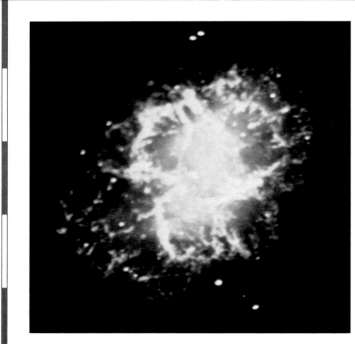

Named "The Crab" because of its appearance in a telescope, the Crab Nebula is a still-expanding cloud of gas. It shines as brightly as 100,000 Suns because its central pulsar emits powerful streams of electrons. Most other star-wrecks are much less luminous.

Pulsars are like lighthouse lamps: as they turn, they send out powerful beams of radiation from hot spots on or just above the surface.

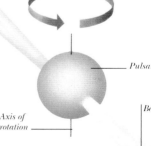

Pulsar

Axis of rotation

Beam of radiation from pulsar

On Earth, we detect a pulse each time a beam of radiation sweeps past us.

THE FATE OF THE SUN

The Sun will swell to a hundred times its present size to swallow Mercury and Venus, and perhaps Earth. Stars like the Sun can squeeze the helium atoms to fuse into carbon, but they do not have enough mass to force the carbon to make any heavier elements. In this type of red giant, the flimsy outer layers swell and shrink and eventually, after a few million years, puff away into space. The resulting smoke ring, known as a planetary nebula, lasts only a few thousand years. All that remains is a collapsed core—a white dwarf—that slowly fades.

STAR CORPSES

When a star dies, its corpse can take three forms (*shown to scale, right*). Most become white dwarfs: superdense stars the size of planets. A massive star may leave behind a heavy core that becomes a neutron star—an object the size of a city but so dense that a pinhead of its matter would weigh a million tonnes. If the core is supermassive, gravity overwhelms it, and it turns into a black hole.

WHITE DWARF

NEUTRON STAR

BLACK HOLE

⑬ AFTERMATH
Even after a supernova, the star's supercollapsed core can survive. It may turn into a pulsar—a rotating neutron star—or a black hole.

Black holes

If a supernova leaves behind a "corpse" at least three times more massive than the Sun, the gravity is so powerful that the corpse shrinks to a point. The pull is immense: to escape you would have to travel at the speed of light. And so the object is black (because light cannot escape), and it is a hole (because nothing can get out after falling in). Black holes may sound like science fiction, but astronomers are confident they have located several left by supernovas.

⑪ END OF THE ROAD
The star then tries to fuse iron, which requires energy instead of giving it out. The star tries to supply this energy by contracting its core still further . . .

⑫ SUPERNOVA
. . . which leads to a massive explosion. The star shines brighter than a billion Suns as it blows itself apart. Gold, platinum, and other rare metals form in the heat and fury of the explosion.

CYGNUS X-1

Black holes are invisible, but they give themselves away if their gravity drags material off a companion star. The snatched material swirls around the hole, getting very hot and giving out X-rays, before disappearing forever. Astronomers think that the best candidate for a black hole in the Milky Way is a powerful source of X-rays in the constellation of Cygnus. This X-ray source, known as Cygnus X-1, is probably a blue supergiant star plus a black hole weighing 10 Suns.

Blue supergiant star

Black hole

Hot spiraling gases

Gas being dragged into black hole

OUR STAR CITY

Imagine a city with 200 billion inhabitants, and so vast that a jumbo jet would take 100 billion years to cross it. We live in such a city: a city of stars known as the Milky Way Galaxy, or just "the Galaxy." Our star city is a huge spiral-shaped collection of stars 100,000 light-years across. The Sun, our local star, is a very minor member of this star city. It is not even in the center, but two-thirds of the way out in the galactic suburbs. "Downtown" is the Galaxy's central bulge, a dense hub of old red and yellow stars. The spiral arms are where star birth is taking place. Studded with young, hot blue stars, the arms are rich in gas and dust—the raw materials of new stars. A halo containing the oldest stars surrounds the whole Galaxy. Although the halo appears to be sparsely populated, astronomers believe it contains lots of invisible "dark matter," which balances the central mass of our star city as it rotates in space.

MAPPING THE MILKY WAY
Astronomers prepared this map of the whole sky by plotting the 7,000 brightest stars in the sky and then adding in nebulas from photographs. It shows how star and gas clouds are concentrated in a flattened disk that appears as a glowing band when seen edge-on. The "holes" in the disk are huge clouds of dust grains, which block the light from the stars behind.

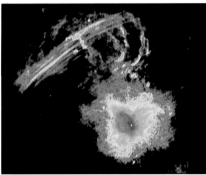

THE GALACTIC CENTER
The central 150 light-years of our Galaxy. This radio image shows an arc of hot gas—perhaps the result of energy generated by a massive black hole at the Galaxy's heart.

ACTIVITIES

● On a moonless night, trace the path of the Milky Way. Because the Galaxy is flattened, the stars are concentrated into a hazy band.

● Find the center of the Galaxy: it is near Scorpius and Sagittarius, where the Milky Way looks brighter.

● Look for the dark patches in the Milky Way—giant dust clouds, which early astronomers thought were "tunnels" in space. Observers in the northern hemisphere should be able to identify the Cygnus Rift, while those in the south should see the Coalsack.

● With binoculars or a small telescope you can see that the Milky Way is made of an enormous number of stars. Many are arranged in loose clusters.

COSMIC SPIRAL
The Milky Way is a typical spiral galaxy. From the side it would look like a pair of fried eggs stuck together back to back (*see below*). The "yolks" form its nucleus or central bulge, while the "whites" form a thin, flattened disk, rich in dust and gas. From above and below, you would be able to see that the material in the disk forms a spiral structure (*see right*). The arms of the spiral, which contain the Galaxy's reserves of gas and dust, are where the youngest stars are concentrated.

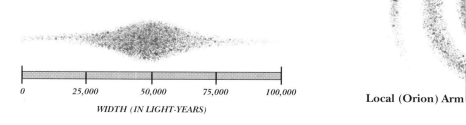

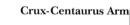
0   25,000   50,000   75,000   100,000
WIDTH (IN LIGHT-YEARS)

Crux-Centaurus Arm

Cygnus Arm

Perseus Arm

Local (Orion) Arm   **Sagittarius Arm**

The Galaxy's outskirts

Billions of years ago, the Milky Way was a huge, round cloud of gas, but it collapsed under the force of its own gravity. This, combined with its spin, made it into the flattened shape we see today. There is, however, a "tidemark" remaining, in the form of the halo, to mark the original extent of our Galaxy. The halo contains the oldest stars in the Galaxy—some are estimated to be 14 billion years old. Many of the stars are found in globular clusters. There are more than 100 clusters in the halo, each a dense ball of hundreds of thousands of stars bound together by gravity.

TOURIST SPOTS IN THE ORION ARM

Name	Distance in light-years	Type	Facts
Hyades	150	Star cluster	200 members; 630 million years old
Betelgeuse	310	Red giant star	Size equal to 400 Suns
Loop I	400	Supernova	Giant bubble 700 light-years across
Coalsack	550	Dark cloud	Mass equal to 40,000 Suns
Rigel	910	Giant star	Blue-white: temperature 20,000°C
Dumbbell Nebula	1,000	Planetary nebula	Width: 2 light-years
Canopus	1,200	Giant star	Brightness equal to 200,000 Suns
Orion Nebula	1,600	Bright nebula	Contains 100 newborn stars
Horsehead Nebula	1,600	Dark nebula	"Nose" to "mane": 4 light-years
Vela Nebula	1,800	Supernova	Age: 11,000 years. Contains pulsar
Epsilon Aurigae	1,900	Double star	One star hidden in huge dark disk
Lacerta OB1	1,900	Star cluster	Stars less than 30 million years old
AE Aurigae	2,000	Young star	Has "run away" from Orion Nebula
Scorpius X-1	2,100	Double star	Powerful source of X-rays
Cygnus Rift	2,400	Dark cloud	Length: 1,500 light-years
Cone Nebula	2,400	Bright nebula	Glowing gas contains dark "cone"
Monoceros R2	2,600	Dark cloud	Newborn stars hidden inside
Camelopardalis OB1	3,000	Star cluster	Stars less than 10 million years old

OUR LOCAL SPIRAL ARM

The Sun lives in the Orion Arm—a "spur," or bridge, between two of the Galaxy's main spiral arms. The map shows a part (about 4,000 by 5,000 light-years) of the Orion Arm containing the Sun, the young stars of Orion, and some of the more famous "tourist spots" in this part of the Galaxy. This is a very active region of star formation, with enormous dust clouds (such as the Cygnus Rift and the Coalsack), nebulas, and young stars. The blue "bubbles" are the remains of young massive stars that exploded as supernovas.

STELLAR BIRTHPLACE
Intense ultraviolet light from the young stars embedded within the Rho Ophiuchi Nebula causes the gas to glow a rich magenta. The blue coloration is due to starlight scattered by dust.

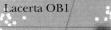
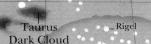

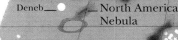

END OF THE ROAD
The Helix Nebula has puffed its red giant envelope into space, revealing a searing hot core at the center—now a shrunken white dwarf star.

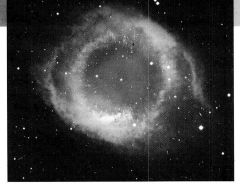

COSMIC COMPANIONS
The Pleiades, born 60 million years ago, still live together as a group. With the naked eye, you can see seven stars (they are sometimes called the Seven Sisters) but there are more than 250 stars in the cluster.

THE LOCAL GROUP

GALAXIES ARE GREGARIOUS OBJECTS. Most do not live alone, but clump together into groups or clusters that are held in place by gravity. Some clusters are enormous: the Virgo Cluster and the Coma Cluster, for example, contain thousands of galaxies occupying areas of up to 20 million light-years across. At the other end of the scale are small groups of galaxies, like the one the Milky Way Galaxy belongs to. This cluster, the Local Group, is a collection of about 30 galaxies scattered over a region of space nearly 5 million light-years across. Its most important members are the Milky Way, the Andromeda Galaxy, and the Triangulum Galaxy M33. The Local Group is just one of the thousands of clusters of galaxies that astronomers have discovered. These clusters, in turn, gather together into loose groups called superclusters—the biggest structures of matter in the Universe, stretching over hundreds of millions of light-years. Our Local Group is a member of the Local Supercluster, which is centered around the Virgo Cluster.

ELLIPTICAL GALAXY
The elliptical galaxies in our Local Group are small and dim. A much more impressive example is M87, which is a member of the Virgo Cluster. It is a huge ball of more than a thousand billion elderly red stars with few new stars. Like all elliptical galaxies, it formed its stars all at once a very long time ago.

IRREGULAR GALAXY
The Small Magellanic Cloud (SMC), like all irregular galaxies, has no obvious shape. Irregular galaxies are also quite small—the SMC has only one-fortieth the mass of the Milky Way. But irregular galaxies are rich in gas and are still actively making new stars. The SMC is one of the closest galaxies to the Milky Way—it may even be a "satellite" of our own—and is easily visible to the unaided eye in the southern hemisphere.

FACTS AND FIGURES

Name of galaxy	Distance (light-years)	Diameter (light-years)	Luminosity (millions of Suns)	Type
Milky Way	0	100,000	15,000	Spiral
Large Magellanic Cloud (LMC)	170,000	30,000	2,000	Irregular spiral
Small Magellanic Cloud (SMC)	190,000	20,000	500	Irregular
Draco	300,000	3,000	0.1	Elliptical
Carina	300,000	3,000	0.01	Elliptical
Sculptor	300,000	6,000	1	Elliptical
Sextans	300,000	3,000	0.01	Elliptical
Ursa Minor	300,000	2,000	0.1	Elliptical
Fornax	500,000	6,000	12	Elliptical
Leo I	600,000	2,000	0.6	Elliptical
Leo II	600,000	2,000	0.4	Elliptical
NGC 6822	1,800,000	15,000	90	Irregular
IC 5152	2,000,000	3,000	60	Irregular
WLM	2,000,000	6,000	90	Irregular
Andromeda	2,200,000	150,000	40,000	Spiral
Andromeda I	2,200,000	5,000	1	Elliptical
Andromeda II	2,200,000	5,000	1	Elliptical
Andromeda III	2,200,000	5,000	1	Elliptical
M32	2,200,000	5,000	130	Elliptical
NGC 147	2,200,000	8,000	50	Elliptical
NGC 185	2,200,000	8,000	60	Elliptical
NGC 205	2,200,000	11,000	160	Elliptical
M33 (Triangulum)	2,400,000	40,000	5,000	Spiral
IC 1613	2,500,000	10,000	50	Irregular
DDO 210	3,000,000	5,000	2	Irregular
Pisces	3,000,000	2,000	0.6	Irregular
GR 8	4,000,000	1,500	2	Irregular
IC 10	4,000,000	6,000	250	Irregular
Sagittarius	4,000,000	4,000	1	Irregular
Pegasus	5,000,000	7,000	20	Irregular
Leo A	5,000,000	7,000	20	Irregular

BARRED SPIRAL GALAXY
NGC 1365, a member of the Fornax Cluster, is a spiral galaxy with a difference. Instead of a central bulge, its old stars are concentrated into a short bar, and the arms emerge from opposite ends of the bar. In a barred spiral, the bar rotates as if it is a solid body—something astronomers find difficult to explain, as it is made of millions of separate stars. It is possible that our Milky Way is a barred spiral galaxy, but we cannot easily tell because we would be seeing the bar edge-on.

Leo A

GR 8

Our corner of the Universe

The Local Group contains about 30 galaxies: probably 3 spirals, 13 irregulars, and 15 ellipticals. The galaxies in our corner of the Universe cluster together in two main clumps: around the Andromeda Galaxy and around the Milky Way. These are the most massive galaxies in the group and have the strongest gravity. Andromeda's clump includes the medium-sized spiral M33, as well as its elliptical companions NGC 205 and M32. The Milky Way is surrounded by the Large and Small Magellanic Clouds, and several dwarf elliptical galaxies. Other dwarf galaxies, especially irregulars such as IC 10 and Leo A, are scattered much more widely. The most abundant type of galaxy in the Local Group are these dim, insignificant dwarfs. They are relatively tiny, containing only a few million stars, but must be the most common galaxies in the Universe. Only those in our immediate neighborhood are close enough to detect, however; distant ones are too dim for even the most powerful of telescopes to spot.

SPINNING CITY

It is obvious from the shape of spiral galaxies that they spin. Careful measurements reveal that they rotate with their arms trailing, but things are not quite that simple. A galaxy is not a solid body and so the stars within it move at different speeds. Apart from the stars in the very center, those in the inner regions circle the galaxy more rapidly than those in the outer regions, and it used to be a mystery why the arms didn't "wind up." Today we think that the spiral arms are areas where stars are densely packed together, like a cosmic traffic jam. Just as a traffic jam persists as individual cars join and escape the jam, so the spiral arm stays the same shape although the individual stars within it are always changing.

ROTATION SPEED

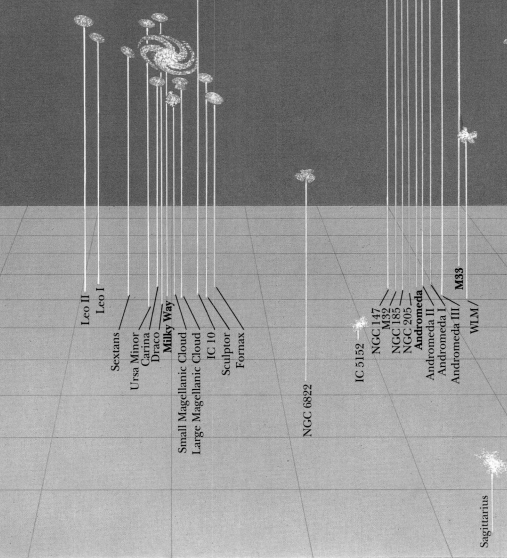

Leo II
Leo I
Sextans
Ursa Minor
Carina
Draco
Milky Way
Small Magellanic Cloud
Large Magellanic Cloud
IC 10
Sculptor
Fornax
NGC 6822
IC 5152
NGC 147
M32
NGC 185
NGC 205
Andromeda
Andromeda II
Andromeda I
Andromeda III
WLM
M33
IC 1613
Pisces
DDO 210
Sagittarius

THE ANDROMEDA GALAXY

At 2 1/4 million light-years away, the Andromeda Galaxy is the most distant object visible to the unaided eye. It is the largest galaxy in the Local Group and, with 400 billion stars, one of the biggest spirals known. Although larger, it is probably very similar to the Milky Way. Unfortunately, we look at it almost edge-on, which makes it difficult for astronomers to study its structure.

ACTIVITIES

● Northern hemisphere: on autumn evenings, away from city lights, find the Andromeda Galaxy (*check the star maps on pages 46–47*). Binoculars reveal just how extensive it is.

● Southern hemisphere: on spring evenings, locate our two closest galaxies, the Large and Small Magellanic Clouds (*see star maps on pages 48–49*). You can spot the Large Cloud even through the haze of city lights.

● Spot our own Galaxy. If you are in a part of the world with a good view of the constellation Sagittarius, look for the widening of the Milky Way. You are looking toward the center of the Galaxy: with a little imagination, you can see that you are viewing a spiral galaxy edge-on from its outskirts.

EXPLODING GALAXIES

GALAXIES ARE NOT ALL PEACEFUL collections of stars. As astronomers probed farther into the Universe, they discovered that some galaxies were extremely disturbed, particularly in their central regions. A few gave out as much energy in the form of radio waves as they did in light. Huge clouds of material surrounded these radio galaxies, thrown out by beams or jets of electrically charged particles spewing from the galaxies' centers. Some, the Seyfert galaxies, had unusually bright centers. And others, the starburst galaxies, had apparently gone through a sudden, massive burst of star formation. Most mysterious of all were quasars. These looked like stars within our Milky Way Galaxy, but even the nearest quasar—3C 273—lies 2,000 million light-years away. The farthest quasars, some 13 billion light-years from us, are the most distant things in the Universe. To be visible at such distances they must be many hundreds of times brighter than normal galaxies. What lies at the heart of these exploding galaxies?

For many years, astronomers believed M82 to be an "active galaxy." Now they know that the spiral galaxy collided with an intergalactic cloud of gas, triggering a violent burst of star birth in the central regions. The red filaments or threads that seem to be shooting out from the center are streams of gas, lit by active young stars falling inward.

Central activity

There are two kinds of exploding galaxy— the active galaxies and the starburst galaxies. The turmoil in an active galaxy is confined to a minuscule part of the central region. In these galaxies, which include radio galaxies, Seyferts, and quasars, the power concentrated in the center is tremendous: many times the energy of the Milky Way in an area the size of the Solar System. Astronomers believe that a supermassive black hole lies at the heart of an active galaxy, surrounded by a raging whirlpool of gas that is spiraling in— the accretion disk. The whirling gas acts like a powerful dynamo, providing the energy that makes the galaxy active. Though they mimic the appearance of active galaxies, starburst galaxies are usually not as violent. Their "activity"—rapid bursts of star birth— results from interactions with nearby galaxies and dust clouds that produce the raw material for stars.

ACCRETION DISK
The source of brilliance in an active galaxy is probably the accretion disk of material swirling into the central black hole. Its glow is so dazzling because it is very hot.

STELLAR SLAUGHTER
Stars close to the black hole are torn apart by the force of its gravity. Their gas becomes part of the accretion disk and eventually spirals into the hole.

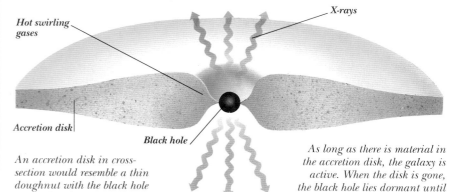

TUNING INTO THE COSMOS

The discovery of exploding galaxies owes a great deal to radio astronomy, a branch of astronomy developed in the 1940s. It involves tuning in to the natural radio waves generated by objects in space. This radiation, like light, can penetrate Earth's atmosphere to reach the surface. Most other wavelengths of radiation —such as X-rays, ultraviolet, and infrared—are blocked by our air, and research into these wavelengths had to await the development of satellites. Astronomers often named radio sources after the con- stellations they appear to lie in. The giant elliptical galaxies Perseus A, Cygnus A, and Hercules A, for example, are radio galaxies. Radio telescopes also discovered pulsars and the radiation left over from the Big Bang.

Part of the VLA—the Very Large Array of radio telescopes—in New Mexico, U.S. Radio telescopes need a larger collecting area than optical telescopes because radio waves have a longer wavelength. The 27 dishes in the VLA act as a 27-km-wide receiver.

THE POWERHOUSE

Defenseless against the powerful gravity of the black hole, the vortex of gas in the accretion disk acts as a dynamo, generating huge amounts of energy. The gas, torn from nearby stars by the force of gravity, swirls in a disk toward the hole. Fiercely heated by friction, the gas shines brilliantly. As well as light, the disk releases other wavelengths of radiation. At the edge of the hole, the gas travels close to the speed of light, and gives off searing X-rays. Beams of electrically charged particles—electrons and protons—shoot out from the inner surface of the disk. Gathering on either side of the galaxy or quasar, these particles create vast clouds, which emit radio waves.

Hot swirling gases

X-rays

Accretion disk

Black hole

An accretion disk in cross- section would resemble a thin doughnut with the black hole as the doughnut hole.

As long as there is material in the accretion disk, the galaxy is active. When the disk is gone, the black hole lies dormant until it receives a fresh supply of gas.

The optical view: *Centaurus A was one of the first radio galaxies to be discovered and, at 16 million light-years, one of the closest. It is a giant elliptical galaxy, with a dark band of dust crossing its central regions. An optical telescope cannot see what lies inside the dust band.*

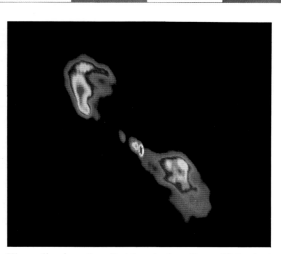

The radio view: *A radio telescope "sees through" the dust to reveal a powerful jet emerging from Centaurus A's core. This jet, moving at about 30,000 km/sec, creates huge, radio-emitting clouds of charged particles around the galaxy. Centaurus A appears to have experienced more than one disturbance. The largest pair of clouds were created millions of years ago; the innermost pair are under construction now. In between, the black hole was dormant—probably because it had run out of gas.*

FEEDING THE MONSTER
Cool gas clouds are reservoirs of material that will spiral into the hole in the future. When there's no more "food," the black hole shuts down.

COSMIC DRAGON
At the center of the accretion disk is the black hole itself. As it gobbles up fresh gas, it is forever increasing in mass, and can "weigh in" at billions of times the mass of the Sun.

SUPERJET
Beams of charged atomic particles—protons and electrons—blast out of the inner accretion disk and scour the surrounding area as they shoot through space at one-tenth the speed of light.

BLACK HOLES
A black hole is a region of space where gravity is so strong that nothing, not even light, can escape. Compared with the black hole created when a supernova explodes (*see page 53*), a black hole at the center of an active galaxy weighs in at the equivalent of *billions* of star-masses. Such supermassive black holes probably formed early in the life of the young galaxy as a result of millions of stars (or their corpses) merging in the crowded central regions. Black holes are famous for sucking everything in, but this is not so. Like any other object, they exert a pull only on their immediate neighborhood. Admittedly the pull is so strong there that it tears the fabric of space apart: anything falling into a black hole disappears from our Universe for good.

The force of gravity is similar to putting a heavy object on a rubber sheet: the "well" in which the object sits attracts other objects to roll toward it. Space itself can be seen as a rubber sheet deformed by many objects of different masses.

A very small and massive object deforms space so much the "rubber sheet" stretches into an infinitely deep well—a black hole.

59

THE UNIVERSE

COSMOLOGY, THE STUDY OF THE UNIVERSE, is a 20th-century science. Until recently, astronomers did not have the tools to probe the Cosmos on its largest scale. Now, with sophisticated telescopes, satellites, and receivers, they can study the history and the geography of our Universe. The Universe is made of galaxies—billions of them. Astronomers estimate that there are 100 billion galaxies, each with 100 billion stars. That is a total of 10,000 million million million stars. The galaxies are not spread out randomly, but organized into clusters of clusters of galaxies—superclusters or "clouds." And these superclusters do not fill the Universe: there are giant empty spaces between them. The Universe's geography also tells its history. When we look at distant galaxies, we see that they are moving apart: the Universe is expanding. If we could "rewind" the Universe, we would see the galaxies moving together and find that our Universe had a definite beginning. Will it then have a definite end?

COBE
The Cosmic Background Explorer satellite probes the radiation created by the birth of the Universe—the Big Bang. At the instant of birth, the temperature of the radiation must have been millions and millions of degrees. COBE's sensors reveal that, with the expansion of the Universe, the radiation has cooled to −270.37° C.

GREAT WALLS
At 300 million light-years from the Milky Way, astronomers have discovered a "Great Wall." This is a line of galaxies curving through space for more than a billion light-years. The Universe may be organized into a series of walls of galaxies, roughly 400 million light-years apart, separated by voids.

Millions of light-years

VOID

VOID

Great Wall of Galaxies

CENTAURUS CLOUD

Local Supercluster

FULL OF HOLES

Astronomers have started mapping the Universe using powerful telescopes to locate tens of thousands of galaxies. The map (*right*) shows an area centered on the Virgo Cluster of galaxies—the heart of our Local Supercluster which spans 100 million light-years. The 31 galaxies of our Local Group form a tiny knot in the distribution of the several thousand galaxies in this region. The superclusters are organized into elongated strings, or filaments, which form the boundaries of huge voids 150–200 million light-years across. On this map, you can see the edge of the voids that butt against the Virgo Supercluster. There may be billions of galaxies, but the Universe is mostly empty, with more void than matter.

OPHIUCHUS CLOUD

SERPENS CLOUD

BOÖTES CLOUD

NGC 5846 Cluster

CANES VENATICI

VIRGO-LIBRA CLOUD

NGC 5371 Cluster

CANES VENATICI SPUR

COMA CLOUD

DRACO CLOUD

COMA-SCULPTOR CLOUD

VIRGO SOUTHERN EXTENSION

Coma Cluster

Ursa Major Cluster

Virgo Cluster

Local Group

Virgo W Cluster

LEO SPUR

CRATER CLOUD

LEO CLOUD

CANCER-LEO CLOUD

ANTLIA-HYDRA CLOUD

Antlia Cluster

0   30   60

MILLIONS OF LIGHT-YEARS

The Big Bang theory

If you could go backward in the history of the expanding Universe, you would come to a time between 15 and 20 billion years ago when all the galaxies were together. That was the instant at which the Universe was born in an unimaginable explosion—the Big Bang. The young Universe must have been an incredibly hot, dense fireball. As the Universe expanded, it cooled, and at some stage—astronomers still don't know exactly when—gas clumped together and the first galaxies were born. Today the Universe is still expanding. The big question is whether we live in an ever-expanding Universe, or if it will eventually collapse in a Big Crunch. Our future rests in the hands of gravity.

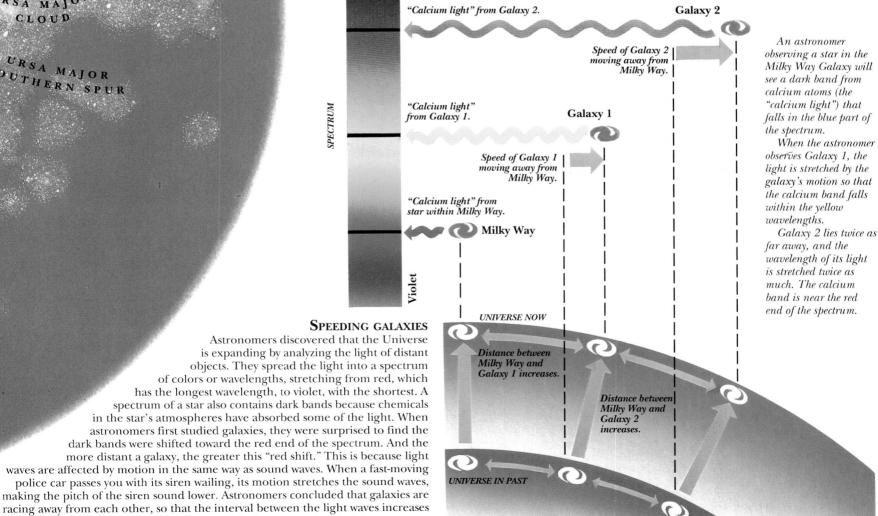

THE EVER-EXPANDING UNIVERSE

If there is not enough material in the Universe to provide gravitational "brakes," then the Universe will expand forever (*as in the top sequence*). The mass of all the galaxies added together falls far short of the amount of matter needed to halt the expansion—and so it looks as if we live in an ever-expanding Universe.

THE BIG CRUNCH

There may, however, be more to the Universe than meets the eye. Astronomers believe it may contain enormous quantities of dark matter—invisible material in an unknown form—to "brake" the expansion. If this is the case, the gravitational pull of the matter would prevent the Universe from growing beyond a certain size, after which gravity would take over and cause the galaxies to collapse (*the lower sequence*). All the matter in the Universe would come together again—this time in a Big Crunch. This might trigger another Big Bang, and the Universe would be reborn—although its makeup and structure would likely be very different from how it is now. Perhaps the Universe never dies, but oscillates between Big Bangs and Big Crunches.

Ever-Expanding Universe

Big Crunch

Big Bang

SHIFT TO THE RED

The expansion of the Universe is carrying all the galaxies away from one another, like spots on the surface of an expanding balloon. The farther apart the galaxies, the faster they are moving apart.

Red

Violet

SPECTRUM

"Calcium light" from Galaxy 2.

Speed of Galaxy 2 moving away from Milky Way.

Galaxy 2

"Calcium light" from Galaxy 1.

Speed of Galaxy 1 moving away from Milky Way.

Galaxy 1

"Calcium light" from star within Milky Way.

Milky Way

An astronomer observing a star in the Milky Way Galaxy will see a dark band from calcium atoms (the "calcium light") that falls in the blue part of the spectrum.

When the astronomer observes Galaxy 1, the light is stretched by the galaxy's motion so that the calcium band falls within the yellow wavelengths.

Galaxy 2 lies twice as far away, and the wavelength of its light is stretched twice as much. The calcium band is near the red end of the spectrum.

SPEEDING GALAXIES

Astronomers discovered that the Universe is expanding by analyzing the light of distant objects. They spread the light into a spectrum of colors or wavelengths, stretching from red, which has the longest wavelength, to violet, with the shortest. A spectrum of a star also contains dark bands because chemicals in the star's atmospheres have absorbed some of the light. When astronomers first studied galaxies, they were surprised to find the dark bands were shifted toward the red end of the spectrum. And the more distant a galaxy, the greater this "red shift." This is because light waves are affected by motion in the same way as sound waves. When a fast-moving police car passes you with its siren wailing, its motion stretches the sound waves, making the pitch of the siren sound lower. Astronomers concluded that galaxies are racing away from each other, so that the interval between the light waves increases and shifts the light reaching Earth toward the long, or red end of the spectrum.

UNIVERSE NOW

Distance between Milky Way and Galaxy 1 increases.

Distance between Milky Way and Galaxy 2 increases.

UNIVERSE IN PAST

CAMELOPARDALIS CLOUD

URSA MAJOR CLOUD

URSA MAJOR SOUTHERN SPUR

MILKY WAY
CENTAURUS A
LEO A
M87
PERSEUS A
GREAT WALL OF GALAXIES
VOID
WALL OF GALAXIES
CYGNUS A
HYDRA A

ARE WE ALONE?

WE KNOW HOW STARS LIVE AND DIE, where planets come from, and even have an idea of how the Universe was born. But what we don't know is whether we are alone in the Universe. At first, it may seem incredible to think of Earth being the only inhabited planet. The Universe contains billions of stars like the Sun; it must surely contain billions of Earthlike planets, too. But we have yet to discover a planet around another star. Even if there were planets, would life necessarily follow? All the other planets in our Solar System are far too hostile—even Mars, the most Earthlike, has not the faintest glimmer of life. Some scientists have worked out that a civilization only slightly more advanced than ours could send robot scout-ships throughout the Galaxy in a few million years—a short time compared to the age of the Galaxy. But, so far, we have yet to find any scientifically convincing evidence of extraterrestrial visitation. Scientists are not very hopeful about finding life in the Universe, but it hasn't stopped them from trying to seek it out. One very exciting area in astronomy is SETI—the Search for Extraterrestrial Intelligence—because the discovery of alien life would be the most important event in the history of the human race.

Star target: the globular cluster M13 is the destination of a message from Earth. In 1974, astronomers used the 305-meter-wide dish of the world's biggest radio telescope at Arecibo, Puerto Rico, to beam a radio message to the dense cluster of stars. M13 is 25,000 light-years away and the message is traveling at the speed of light, so we cannot expect a reply for 50,000 years.

EARTH AND THE MOON

MOON MEMORIAL
The Apollo 11 astronauts left behind a plaque commemorating the first journey by humans to another world. It is signed by the three crew members—Neil Armstrong, Buzz Aldrin, and Mike Collins—and U.S. President Richard Nixon.

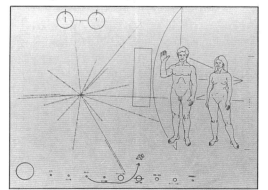

ONE SMALL STEP
We have not traveled far in search of life in the Universe. Twelve astronauts have walked on the Moon, but it is a mere hop in space terms—only 384,000 km. By comparison Mars, at its closest, is 200 times farther off, and a round-trip would take at least two years. Astronauts could carry out a more detailed search for life than robot craft, but as there is almost certainly no life elsewhere in the Solar System, they would have to travel to other star systems to seek it out. With current spacecraft the journey would last many lifetimes.

SOLAR SYSTEM

FOR ALIEN EYES
An alien finding the plaque carried on the two Pioneers could work out a lot about its makers, including where we come from and what we look like.

THE NEXT FRONTIER
We have now explored all the planets (and several of their moons) in close-up, except for Pluto. None of our neighbors shows any sign of life. Living things must be based on carbon, the only element that can build up the complex structures of life. The other essential ingredient is water to dissolve the chemicals that fuel life's processes. In the Solar System, liquid water exists only on Earth. Four spacecraft are now leaving the Solar System and journeying across the Galaxy. In case aliens should stumble across our spacecraft, they carry messages from Earth. *Pioneers 10* and *11* have an engraved plaque (*left*) while *Voyagers 1* and *2* carry a long-playing record (*right*) with many typical "Sounds of Earth," including greetings in 55 languages.

A UNIVERSE TEEMING WITH LIFE?

From the number of stars in our Galaxy and an estimate of the proportion that may have Earthlike planets, astronomers can guess how many civilizations exist in the Milky Way. The estimates range from 10 million to one. But our Galaxy is just one of billions. Surely, among all those clusters, superclusters, and filaments making up the Universe, there *must* be life. There might be—but it may be so far away that we can never meaningfully communicate with it—after all, the Sun and planets are relative latecomers compared with many stars. Or it may be a life form so different from us that we have nothing in common. The question of life is the one question about the Universe we cannot answer: we just have to wait and see.

LOCAL SUPERCLUSTER

MESSAGE TO THE UNKNOWN

Our first deliberate signal to aliens, the Arecibo message, is traveling toward M13, one of the globular clusters in the halo of our Milky Way Galaxy. Astronomers have no evidence that there is anyone there to receive it, but with 500,000 stars in the cluster there is a slim chance. The message consists of a string of 1,679 on-off, or binary, commands, which a mathematically minded alien could arrange to create a picture (*see right*). This shows, among other things, our number system, the basis of life, an outline of a human and of the Arecibo telescope, and Earth's place in the Solar System. The message is not a serious attempt at communication, but an exercise in working out how aliens might talk to each other.

MILKY WAY

M13

ARECIBO MESSAGE
The radio message to M13 consists of 1,679 on-off commands: 1,679 being the result of multiplying 23 by 73. On arranging the commands into a 23 x 73 rectangle, a "picture" emerges.

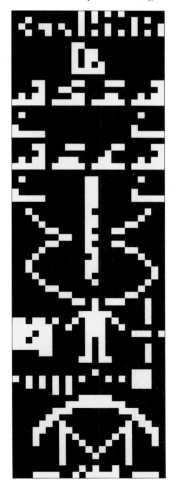

NEARBY STARS

1920

1936

1962

1976

Viking

Telstar

First public television broadcast

First regular radio broadcast

BROADCASTING OUR PRESENCE

We have been unintentionally broadcasting our presence for many years. The radio waves carrying our radio and television programs are not confined to Earth; they leak away into space. Traveling at the speed of light, these radio waves are spreading out through the Galaxy. Those from the first radio broadcasts in the 1920s have now passed all the stars within about 70 light-years of the Sun, while the signals carrying the first TV programs have reached 60 light-years. Star systems closer than this will have picked up other transmissions—such as those between Earth and the *Viking* Landers on Mars in 1976. Likewise, radio telescopes on Earth could detect "leaked" broadcasts from planets circling other stars; but so far, they have not found any.

FROM TELSTAR TO VEGA
The Telstar *satellite made history in August 1962 when it transmitted the first live TV pictures between the U.S. and Europe. Telstar was only 90 cm in diameter, but the signals from this historic broadcast reached the star Vega in 1988.*

INDEX

ACKNOWLEDGMENTS

Dorling Kindersley would like to thank:
Richard Czapnik for designing the
initial stages of the book; Hilary Bird
for compiling the index; Anna Kunst
for translating

Picture Research Diana Morris

Picture credits
(t=top, c=center, b=bottom, r=right,
l=left)

Photographs
© **Anglo–Australian Telescope Board**
photos, David Malin: 55bl and cover
(1979); 56c (1987); 56cb (1991); 59tc
(1980)
Lund Observatory: Martin Keskǔla and
Tatjana Keskǔla 54tr
NASA: 7tr, 8tr, 12tr, 14tl, 26tl, 27bc &
cover, 38tl, 42tl, 50tr, 62cl, 62bl
Jet Propulsion Laboratory/NASA: 25tl,
25cr, 29cr, 34tl & cover, 34br, 35tr, 37tr

McDonnell Douglas: 9br
Picturepoint: 4cl
© **Royal Observatory, Edinburgh &
Anglo–Australian Telescope Board:**
photos, David Malin: 50cl & cover, 55cr
(1979), 55br (1985)
Science Photo Library: Earth Satellite
Corporation 10tl; 11tl; George East
16tl, 17tr; Fred Espenak 5tr; Hale
Observatories 43tr; Jean Lorre 58tr;

NASA 22tl, 24tl, 28cl, 30tl, 32tl, 36tl,
57cr, 62br; NOAO 52bl; Novosti 25br;
NRAO/AUI 54cl, 59tr; Roger
Ressmeyer, Starlight 58 br; Ronald
Royer 40tl & cover, 50b, 56tc; John
Sanford 41bl, U.S. Geological Survey
28tl, U.S. Naval Observatory 62tr
Telegraph Colour Library: 5cr, 63bl

Artwork: Martyn Foote 63br